Nurturing Sustainable Prosperity in West Africa

"This book is an interesting introduction to the ways in which culture influences economic growth and productivity in Ghana. Using a combination of revealing anecdotes and citations from the literature Dr. Armah explores the ways that culture can positively, and negatively, impact the institutions that are necessary to allow a country to thrive. Aspects of culture that are a hindrance cannot be changed immediately, but can, over time, adapt to improve the country."
—Erik Cheever, Professor, *Department of Engineering, Swarthmore College*

"An easy and thought provoking read! It contains a bold message that I expect will facilitate an important conversation not only in Ghana but across Africa."
—Saweda Liverpool-Tasie, *Associate Professor of Agricultural, Food, and Resource Economics, Michigan State University*

"Armah's thesis is that corruption, economic inefficiency, and weak formal institutions are culturally rooted in Ghana, and that the real work of development involves changing the worldviews that give life events their meaning and determine how people respond to formal policies and institutions. This is a controversial argument that will provoke lively debate. Armah's book puts the literature on economic development and culture into dialogue with stories of life in post-independence Ghana."
—Stephen A. O'Connell, Gil and Frank Mustin, *Professor of Economics, Swarthmore College*

"I have no doubt that culture, in terms of attitudes, values, norms and behavior, is the single most important explanatory factor in Ghana's underdevelopment. It explains the widespread corruption, poor work ethic and indiscipline. These are the issues Stephen Armah courageously takes on in this book as needing to be addressed in Ghana's development."
—Stephen Adei, *Professor Emeritus, Ashesi University*

"Stephen Armah's *Nurturing Sustainable Prosperity in West Africa* explores and interprets the economics, transnational organizations, socio-cultural politics as contexts and processes for understanding corruption in Ghana, in particular and Africa as a whole. Focusing on the continuous transactions among Ghanaians with reference to their social and personal obligations against the backdrop of the pervasive corruption exemplified in his case studies, Armah clearly explains the process of constructing socio-political mores and policies to remedy or root out chronic corruption. Armah examines the institutionalized and non-formal customary practices that engender nepotism, absenteeism, lawlessness and general malaise that hamper development. The book provides an important analysis and solutions to corruption. It will be of interest to not only to scholars of economics but also, to the general reader, policymakers and servant- leaders in contemporary Africa."

—Pashington Obeng, *Dean of the Faculty of Arts and Science, Ashesi University*

Stephen Armah

Nurturing Sustainable Prosperity in West Africa

Examples from Ghana

Stephen Armah
Ashesi University College
Berekuso, Ghana

ISBN 978-3-030-37489-1   ISBN 978-3-030-37490-7 (eBook)
https://doi.org/10.1007/978-3-030-37490-7

© The Editor(s) (if applicable) and The Author(s) 2020
This work is subject to copyright. All rights are solely and exclusively licensed by the Publisher, whether the whole or part of the material is concerned, specifically the rights of translation, reprinting, reuse of illustrations, recitation, broadcasting, reproduction on microfilms or in any other physical way, and transmission or information storage and retrieval, electronic adaptation, computer software, or by similar or dissimilar methodology now known or hereafter developed.
The use of general descriptive names, registered names, trademarks, service marks, etc. in this publication does not imply, even in the absence of a specific statement, that such names are exempt from the relevant protective laws and regulations and therefore free for general use.
The publisher, the authors and the editors are safe to assume that the advice and information in this book are believed to be true and accurate at the date of publication. Neither the publisher nor the authors or the editors give a warranty, expressed or implied, with respect to the material contained herein or for any errors or omissions that may have been made. The publisher remains neutral with regard to jurisdictional claims in published maps and institutional affiliations.

This Palgrave Pivot imprint is published by the registered company Springer Nature Switzerland AG.
The registered company address is: Gewerbestrasse 11, 6330 Cham, Switzerland

I dedicate this book to Natalie and Charlotte Armah as well as Priscilla, Jake, Jason and Sean Okaiteye, who are my nieces and nephews. Uncle Steve says always reach for the skies.

Preface

In 1991 my family moved from Nsawam to Accra, the capital of Ghana. This move made me very angry and left me confused because I had to leave my friends and the familiarity of Nsawam, a small town with a close-knit people that I called my home to the big city. I did not want to readjust to a different culture. I was comfortable where I was. I knew all my neighbors, and everyone seemed to know and love me. I did not see the point of moving to the capital with its very impersonal culture and mean-spiritedness.

My older sisters Susan and Jasmin, who were in university at the time, and my elder brother, Joseph, who was in secondary school, seemed to get it. I did not get it and protested loudly to no avail. However, as my parents explained, we were Ga's from Accra, and even though work had taken my parents to Nsawam, and I had essentially been born during this period, it was time to return to our roots. An interesting caveat is that my parents had inadvertently ensured that I suffered no problems with identity in choosing my place of birth. I was born at the Korle Bu teaching hospital in Accra even though my parents were not living in Accra at the time as it was the premier teaching hospital in the country at the time.

Looking back, I admit that my parents made the right choice. Ghana was undergoing significant change at the time with rural-urban migration starting to heat up as the urban centers of Ghana began to develop. In 1992, the very next year, Flight Lt. Rawlings, who had ruled Ghana as a benign dictator for more than a decade, handed over power to himself as an elected democratic leader. At the time, Ghana had primarily state institutions because of a heritage of socialism with a small formal private sector but a large informal sector. The military was a prominent part of our lives as Ghanaians, ensuring disciplined behavior mostly through the tacit threat of corporal punishment.

The change to democracy brought with it a significant loosening of state control with liberalization of the banking sector, the telecom sector, the health sector and so on. However, it took time for any changes to be made in the educational sector. Ghana only had three universities at the time, which were all state owned and in a bad state with overcrowded classrooms and decaying infrastructure. Access to university education was also severely limited as population pressure in the presence of inelastic supply severely stressed the resources of universities.

As I progressed through my high school education, I resolved to travel abroad to obtain higher education because I could see first-hand the state of the country's universities. The situation was so bad that as a student at Presbyterian Senior Secondary School (PRESEC), which was located close to the University of Ghana, I could attend university lectures at N-Block at University of Ghana and the students would not even notice that I was not a university student. There were just too many of them in a classroom which even though was large could not contain the numbers.

I subsequently traveled to the USA for my university education, attending elite universities including Swarthmore College for my undergraduate degree, Emory University for a Master's degree and the University of Illinois at Urbana-Champaign for my Doctorate. However, throughout my studies in the USA, my passion for development never waned. Anyone who has spoken to me for more than 10 minutes will attest to the fact that my passion for African development runs deep and my determination to see my own country, Ghana, prosper is intense because the country is exceptionally well endowed with both natural and human resources. However, there is nothing sycophantic about my love for my country. I am not afraid to criticize aspects of Ghanaian behavior that I find counterproductive to development as this book attests to. However, I am quick to offer credit where credit is due.

I first generated the idea for this book in 2012, subsequent to President Barack Obama's visit to Ghana. I had been publishing many articles on foreign aid but following Obama's advice to Africa in Accra when he visited that "Africa needs strong institutions not strong leaders," I began to entertain the idea that the answer to African development may lie with Africans.

I had been teaching development economics at Ashesi University in Ghana for several years emphasizing the role of formal economic and political institutions in the spirit on Douglas North as well as Daron Acemoglu and his co-authors. Of course, I was not pleased that Obama had tried to pass off the ideas of North Acemoglu and Johnson and others as his own, but that story is for another day. At the least Obama should have acknowledged the source of his advice.

On another front, I was a lecturer at Ashesi, and Ashesi University's curriculum strongly emphasized leadership as an essential ingredient in educating young people. In fact, Patrick Awuah, Ashesi's president, insisted that Africa's problems were so dire that strong leadership was the only thing that could make a difference. Awuah was not referring to dictators or "strong leaders" as Obama had called them but to well-educated leaders with integrity who knew what to do and were not afraid to do the right thing.

I realized that both Obama and Awuah were right; Africa's problems need an African solution. However, strong institutions and effective leaders will not naturally emerge out of thin air. Especially if the culture of the people were such that the opportunity cost of doing the right thing was high for leaders and existing institutions were already weak, something had to give.

As difficult as it is to criticize the culture of a people since value systems tend to be different, I realized that productivity-enhancing habits, traits, norms and beliefs go a long way in the development process and in complementing the efforts of leaders. Such traits also make it possible for strong institutions to emerge that can help perpetuate productivity-enhancing behaviors and activities.

I have also come to the realization that just as the economics literature ignored the question of culture as a determinant of development, economic advice from Western scholars to Africa always side-step the question of culture. This is a fundamental mistake as culture is so important to the African. The failure of economic policies to deliver on impactful developmental objectives only goes to substantiate the hardline views of some Africanists that Western-trained economists "do not get it" and that market economics just does not work in Africa.

I respectfully disagree and rather insist that since countries that recently developed and lifted millions out of poverty (Singapore, China, Hong-Kong and even the UAE) engaged with culture shock and often had to make painful cultural adjustment to fully integrate into the global market and develop, the issue of culture is not a trivial one. In particular, if the forces of globalization are indeed inevitable, then Africans have to face the question of culture's impact on development and how to take advantage of cultural dynamics in the development process.

This book emerged out of several years of engaging with the interactions between culture and development through my research, teaching and lived experience. The book is written for everyone interested in the real development of Africa and not just lip-service. It is written for Africans and for all lovers of Africa, African policymakers and everyone who want to see Africa progress.

Berekuso, Ghana   Stephen Armah
November 2019

Acknowledgment

"Ubuntu" is a famous African philosophy, which reflects the philosophical leanings of the African's world view. Among other things, ubuntu embodies communalism, humanness and the common good of society. This philosophy maintains that the success of the individual, and the community at large, depends on teamwork, collective effort, interdependence and support toward a common goal. Ubuntu says that "I am because you are" interpreted as the success of the individual depends not solely on themselves but also on others around him or her. Albert Einstein, though not an African, clearly espoused "Ubuntu" when he declared that "if I have seen far, it is because I have stood on the shoulders of giants."

I developed the idea for the book several years ago after teaching at Ashesi University in Ghana. I had spent more than 15 years prior to that in the USA as an undergraduate student at Swarthmore College, a graduate student at Emory University and a PhD student cum economics instructor at University of Illinois at Urbana—Champaign. At each of these institutions that I attended, exceptional people stepped up to assist me on my academic journey. From Swarthmore, I thank Eric Cheever, Stephen O'Connell, Amanda Bayer, Ahamindra Jain, Farouk Siddiqui and Arthur McGarity among others. From Emory University, I thank Jerry Thursby and Mahmhut Yassar for their fatherly advice. I acknowledge the contributions of Phil Garcia, Carl Nelson, Alex Winter-Nelson, Paul McNamara and Melvin Wagner all from the University of Illinois at Urbana—Champaign. They all helped to make me who I am today. How can I forget Master Obeng and Mr. Obeney both of Nana Osae Djan

Experimental LA Primary and both of blessed memory? They sowed in me a seed of excellence by insisting that "Only the best is good enough."

However, the successful completion of this book is as a result of the support and significant contribution of several people, who I will now acknowledge. Without a doubt my biggest motivation has come from my family, the Armahs of North Kaneshie (my dad and mum and my siblings Susan, Jasmin and Joseph). However, Joseph stands out in his contribution in hosting me during my stays in the USA and for always pushing me to pursue excellence. My profound gratitude also goes to my lifelong friend and chief motivator Nalwanda Shamutete of Facebook company in California and formerly of Amazon.

I will like to thank my dad, Mr. Mathew Eric Armah, for critical analysis of my thinking concerning Ghanaian culture and for pushing me "to get the whole story." I would also like to thank Atarebono Amwelmoo and Nina Chachu both of Ashesi University who both read through the manuscript and helped me with various suggestions. I will also like to recognize and acknowledge these individuals from Ashesi University for their insightful feedback toward the completion of this book: Prof. Angela Owusu-Ansah, Prof. Pashington Obeng, Dr. Enyonam Candace Kudonoo, Miss Esther Laryea, Mr. Prince Baah, Mr. Alhassan Affum and Mr. Stephen Gyan. Your inputs and suggestions made this book such a success. A very special thank you also goes to Miss Yasmin Bucknor, Chief Operating Officer at Ashesi, for steadfast support and encouragement to finish the book.

I would like to acknowledge the following faculty and members of the Economics Department at Denison University for different suggestions concerning the book: Luis Villa Nueva, Andrea Ziegert and Sohrab Behdad. I also recognize the entire Westmoreland family at Granville, Ohio.

Many thanks also to Prof. Philip Jefferson and Prof. Erik Cheever both of Swarthmore College for their encouragement. I would also like to acknowledge and thank Miss Atarebono Amwelmoo and Miss Elona Boateng, who devoted time and effort into researching, proof reading, editing and referencing of this book. I could not have done it without your assistance.

Finally, a special thank you to my 2019 Development Economic students at Ashesi. Your strong and passionate arguments and critical analysis of the complexity of the Ghanaian culture and how it builds or weakens institutions strongly influenced this book. I am impressed by all of you. Thanks also to the generations of development economics students at Ashesi from 2010 to 2018.

Helen Keller once said, "Alone we can do so little, together we can do so much," and this has certainly been my experience throughout the research process and writing of this book.

Stephen Armah

Contents

1 Introduction   1

2 An Interesting Story on Ghanaian Behavior   7

3 A Review of the Culture: Institutions Nexus   21

4 Corruption and Culture in Ghana: Mission Impossible or an Interesting Challenge   35

5 Concluding Remarks   83

Bibliography   87

Index   101

About the Author

Stephen Armah is a development economist and is Senior Lecturer and Head of the Department of Business Administration at Ashesi University in Berekuso, Ghana. Apart from being the Senior editor of Ashesi's only academic journal, the *Ashesi Economic Lecture Series Journal*, Armah is also the institution's Liaison for the Global Liberal Arts Alliance (GLAA). Armah serves as the founder and director of the Ashesi Economics Lecture Series, Ashesi's first lecture series, and is also the Faculty Lead for capstone research in the Business Administration Department at Ashesi.

Armah is an experienced academic with over 18 years of experience, teaching at the college level. He has taught more than 50 different college courses since 2001 mostly in economics, development and leadership-related subjects. Armah is also an experienced researcher with over 20 publications and more than a 200 conference presentation to his name apart from successfully supervising over 50 undergraduate theses, over 130 masters' theses and a few PhD theses. Armah has also traveled and presented research at more than 30 different institutions in more than 15 different countries in Europe, Asia, North America and Africa.

In terms of his formal education, Armah attended Nana Osae Djan experimental LA primary in Nsawam, where he served as school prefect and won numerous prizes. He then proceeded to Adisadel College in Cape Coast, Ghana, where he was well known for sweeping countless academic prizes. After Adisadel College, Armah proceeded to Presbyterian Boys Secondary School (Presec) in Legon, Accra, Ghana, where he again excelled and won a prize on his graduation. Armah then attended Swarthmore college in the USA for his undergraduate education. He then obtained a masters' degree at Emory University and a PhD from the University of Illinois at Urban-Champaign in the Department of Applied and Consumer Economics.

Armah has won many awards for his research and teaching. Armah was recognized by Ashesi for his teaching and dedication in 2014 and won awards for supervising masters' theses as well. In terms of research he won the top paper at the "Africa in the Age of Globalization" Conference held at Simon Laurier University in Brantford, Ontario, Canada, in 2010. He won the Ralph Joseph Mutti Dissertation Award, at the University of Illinois at Urbana-Champaign in 2009. He won the Best Doctoral Research Award, at the First International Business Conference, held at Dearborn, MI in 2008. He was recognized by the University of Illinois Graduate School for Significant Leadership in an Academic Discipline in 2009. He also won the award for the best graduate student paper at the Southwestern Economics paper contest in 2008 held in New Orleans, Louisiana. He also won the award for the best Graduate Student Paper, at the Illinois Economics Association Graduate Student Paper Contest in 2008.

At University of Illinois, Armah was made a member of Gamma Sigma Delta in recognition for High Achievement in Agriculture, in 2006. At Emory university, Armah won a graduate fellowship from 2001 to 2003. At Swarthmore College, Armah won the Black Cultural Center's Directors' award for Leadership in 2001. He also won the Scott B. Lily Award for academic excellence from 2001 to 2003. Armah is the last of the children of Mr. and Mrs. M.E.A. Armah.

CHAPTER 1

Introduction

Abstract This chapter identifies tardiness as a cultural trait that has impact for Ghana's development. It discusses how traditional Ghanaian reverence of leaders which absolves these leaders from being timely may be out of touch with current pressures for efficiency. Modern demands for economic fulfillment require leaders to lead by example in the quest for efficiency which demands timeliness. The chapter also evaluates Huntington's (*Political Order in Changing Societies*. New Haven: Yale University Press, 2000) claim that the difference in performance between South Korea and Ghana in the 1960s–1990s period was due to perverse Ghanaian cultural practices. It concludes that while culture matters it is probably not the only dynamic at play.

Keywords Economic development • Tardiness • Efficiency • Ghana and South Korea

In a 2018 British Broadcasting Corporation (BBC) article, Elizabeth Ohene, a former Ghanaian government official during the 2000–2008 regime of President John Agyekum Kufuor of Ghana, discusses how in Ghana, the cultural expectation is that the citizenry must be late for both formal and informal events whether in business or in governance.

Ohene discusses the mayhem and embarrassment that emerged when as a presidential staffer, she tried to ensure that President Kufuor will get

© The Author(s) 2020
S. Armah, *Nurturing Sustainable Prosperity in West Africa*,
https://doi.org/10.1007/978-3-030-37490-7_1

to functions that he had been invited to on time. Interestingly, no one was prepared for a timely Ghanaian president and no one expected President Kufuor to be on time for these functions. It was unprecedented for Ghanaian leaders to be on time, so foreign diplomats and Ghanaians alike were rattled by the president's promptness. The commencement of functions attended by the president were therefore chaotic, as unprepared hosts, foreign and local, faced a president who was on time but was not expected to be on time.

Tardiness or the inability to be timely is just one of the several traits of Ghanaians that can be argued to undermine productivity. In fact, Adei and Armah (2018) reported that Ghana's economy, especially the public sector, suffered severely from low productivity. They noted that despite being a significantly smaller neighbor and one of the smallest countries in Africa, Togo's public sector was significantly much more productive than Ghana's. Productivity-sapping traits are clearly considered in a negative light, and there appears to be several other negative productivity-sapping traits that plague Ghanaians as identified by Huntington (2000).

Huntington (2000) chanced across and compared data from Ghana and South Korea in the early 1970s. He was struck by the similarity in the structures of the economies of these independent developing countries in terms of income per capita as measured by real GDP per capita, the severity of inflation, size of population, types of exports and level of foreign aid received and so on.

However, when he compared the same two countries several years later in the 1990s, he found that while South Korea had metamorphosed into an industrialized, first world country, Ghana had barely changed. South Korea's GDP per capita was now 15 times greater than that of Ghana. This observation encouraged Huntington to comment, in surprising endorsement of Max Webber's (1930) Protestant ethic that "while South Koreans valued thrift, investment, hard work, education, organization, and discipline, Ghanaians had different values" (Huntington 2000). Huntington attributed the difference in performance to a difference in culture.

Huntington (2000) argued that culture matters and the main reason for Ghana's developmental struggle was a perverse culture that did not enhance wealth creation. In contrast, South Korean culture emphasized and valued pro-market wealth creation values like "education, investment, thrift, hard work, organization, and discipline." This enabled South Korea to forge ahead and grow rapidly while Ghana was held back by cultural values that were antimarket and counterproductive.

According to Claros and Perotti (2014) the issue with Huntington's (2000) honest but politically incorrect statement is that it suggests that Ghanaians live beyond their means, are indolent, ignorant, disorganized and undisciplined.

Even if true, such a statement will fail to elicit a useful conversation with Ghanaian leaders about how to replicate Korea's success (Heffner 2002). This may be even more relevant if, instead of culture, the actual drag on development is some other factor that is correlated with both culture and development or just appears to be cultural in nature.

Irrespective of Huntington's (2000) observations and conclusions about Ghana, what may also be true is that culture is dynamic not static so just because Huntington noticed a culture in Ghana that was not supportive of wealth creation at the time he wrote his observations does not mean that Ghanaians' culture is set in stone and cannot adapt to change. I am in no way claiming that Huntington (2000) implied Ghana was doomed to poverty and mediocrity because of its perverse culture, but it is worth noting that culture can change based on external influences such as globalization and education and in response to competing values and effective leadership.

Further, although, like Huntington, I am a firm believer that culture matters, and I do think that culture explains, at least in part, some of Ghana's developmental challenges, a comparison of the trajectory of South Korean and Ghanaian development, subsequent to Huntington's (2000) comments, casts at least a little doubt on, though it does not discredit, Huntington's (2000) hypothesis that culture was the primary factor holding Ghana back from achieving its developmental objectives.

Culture was, and probably still is, a major drag on Ghana's development, but there are probably a myriad of other factors as well responsible for Ghana's below par performance that Huntington observed. This fact is in some ways illustrated by what has happened to Ghana and South Korea subsequent to Huntington's writings.

From 1992 to 2018, the real GDP per capita of Ghana's economy has expanded faster than 5% on a year-ago basis for the entire 26 years achieving world record growth rates of 14% in 2011 following the discovery of oil in Ghana. Ghana's GDP per capita which was 15 times lower than South Korea's GDP at the time Huntington was writing is still 15 times smaller than South Korea's GDP today.

On the surface the fact that Ghana GDP per capita is still 15 times smaller than South Korea's in 2019, exactly like it was a generation ago in the 1990s, appears to confirm Huntington's (2000) implied hypothesis that Ghanaian culture did not value pro-market wealth creation attributes like *investment, hard work, education,* and *organization.* The chain of events subsequent to Huntington's observation, however, masks a lot of dynamism in Ghana's, South Korea's and the global economy from the 1990s to the 2100s.

A hypothetical example will make things clear. Recall that the GDP per capita of South Korea was already substantially large in the 1990s compared to Ghana. If Ghana's economy were initially much smaller and stalling because of perverse cultural factors, Ghana's average incomes will be significantly lower than South Korean incomes at the present times instead of maintaining a constant phase difference with it.

Rather, what has happened since the 1990s is that even though both Ghanaian and South Korean GDP are both significantly higher in real terms than they were a generation ago, Ghanaian incomes have quadrupled while South Korean incomes have only doubled at best. Further, there has been the emergence of a new middle class in Ghana with access to first world facilities including the latest malls, high-rise buildings, gated apartment communities, new stadia, airport and rail systems.

Clearly, Ghanaians retain some, if not most, of the negative cultural traits that Huntington noticed and documented. However, Ghanaians do have several positive traits as well such as a love for foreigners, tribal, religious and political tolerance, an entrepreneurial spirit, often inhibited by a lack of access to capital, significant and palpable media freedom, and a genuine interest in sustaining the peace which must in some way account for some of the moderate progress the country has made recently. In fact, according to a May 19, 2019, CNN report, the International Monetary Fund (IMF) projects that Ghana will record fastest rate of economic growth in the whole world for 2019 which is no mean feat.

Tardiness, however, is a particularly poignant example of a productivity-sapping trait as it has a cultural basis. This means even though Huntington did not mention tardiness explicitly as one of Ghana's negative cultural traits, his stress on inefficiency is not misplaced. Further, even though historically, different tribes in Ghana, for example, the Akan, did observe ritualized events and observed a calendar of festivals (see Adjaye 1987), accurate observation of time especially by traditional rulers was relative.

My conversations with traditional leaders have led to my understanding of the cultural underpinning of this behavior that will be strange to a Westerner. In particular, the prestige of traditional rulers in Ghana includes a need for all others to "wait for them" and to greet them once they sit. What will be the point of an impressive ritualized entrance of a chief if subjects were not already sitting down when he enters but rather he enters with them. This same expectation was extended to the seat of the presidency after independence and may explain why the citizenry of Ghana and even foreign dignitaries do not expect leaders to be on time.

The consequence of a lack of respect by leaders for time is that it percolates down the leadership chain to the citizens and followers because they develop an expectation that they need not be on time. Such an expectation may develop into a culture that seeps through the conduct of affairs of production, business and politics, and may undermine productivity by sustaining a culture of tardiness, undermining productivity and stalling growth.

Even more interesting is that culture has been identified in the current economic literature to impact institutions and to be impacted by institutions in determining developmental outcomes (Roland 2016). This is an interesting fact as even though cultural economics is now enjoying the most intensive scrutiny by contemporary economics, for the longest time, economics avoided the analysis of culture even as it welcomed and was dominated by institutional economics championed by North (1990) and later Acemoglu, Johnson and Robinson.

A cultural practice that weakens institutions and is itself affected negatively by the weakened institutions will lead to a perverse developmental outcome of a vicious cycle of poverty guaranteeing that such a people will be forever mired in poverty. In contrast, a cultural practice that strengthens institutions and is itself propped up by the strong institutions will lead to a desirable developmental outcome of a virtuous cycle of prosperity guaranteeing that such a people will forever live the good life.

Of course, culture changes slowly, but culture is dynamic and can change in the presence of new information. However, how can this new information credibly impact culture, which in turn will strengthen institutions leading to a virtuous cycle of prosperity instead of a vicious cycle of poverty? Answering such a question by appealing to specific examples in Ghana is the focus of this book. I acknowledge the work of Nnadozie and Afeikhena (2019) for the general African case but argue that its relevance for Ghana is valuable but limited. We recognize that the relationship between institutions and culture in determining developmental outcomes is non-linear, interdependent and interconnected. Tardiness is not the only characteristic of Ghanaians that is supposed to be at variance with productivity. The list is extensive, and we discuss the details in the next chapter.

Bibliography

Adei, S., & Armah, S. E. A. (2018). *"Ghana Beyond Aid" and What It Will Take to Achieve It*. Paper Presented at Ashesi Econ Lecture Series, Norton-Motulsky Hall, King Engineering Building, Ashesi University, Berekuso, E/R, Ghana.

Adjaye, J. K. (1987). Time, the Calendar, and History Among the Akan of Ghana. *The Journal of Ethnic Studies, 15*(3), 71.

Huntington, S. (2000). *Political Order in Changing Societies*. New Haven: Yale University Press.

Lopez-Claros, A., & Perotti, V. (2014). *Does Culture Matter for Development?* Policy Research Working Paper No. WPS 7092. Washington, DC: World Bank Group.

Nnadozie, E., & Afeikhena, J. (Eds.). (2019). *African Economic Development*. New York: Emerald Publishers.

North, D. (1990). *Institutions, Institutional Change, and Economic Performance*. New York: Cambridge University Press.

Roland, G. (2016, January). *Culture, Institutions and Development*. Namur January 2016 Conference.

Weber, M. (1930). *The Protestant Ethic and the Spirit of Capitalism*. New York: Scribner.

CHAPTER 2

An Interesting Story on Ghanaian Behavior

Abstract This chapter paints a picture of contemporary Ghanaian life as presented to a foreign tourist. Traditional Ghanaian practices such as weddings and funerals are vividly described. Further certain perplexing outcomes such as indiscipline in the siting and construction of houses as well as the unruly behavior of drivers on Ghana's roads are discussed. Some of the negative observations juxtaposed against a very empathetic world view of Ghanaians that unfortunately may itself nurture corruption.

Keywords Corruption • Weddings • Funerals • Corruption and empathy

Imagine your first visit to Ghana as a foreigner from a large city in a developed, first world country. You may be American from New York, Canadian from Toronto, Australian from Sydney, British from London, European from Paris, Chinese from Shanghai or Japanese from Tokyo. You have been told and read several stories of Ghana being a gentle introduction to West Africa. A peaceful country in a region considered to be one of the most impoverished in the world.

For the sake of this story, imagine you are in Ghana because you are attending the wedding ceremony of your college roommate from the college you attended and graduated from in the USA 15 years ago as an international student. You are in your 30s, earn a good income and are no

© The Author(s) 2020
S. Armah, *Nurturing Sustainable Prosperity in West Africa*,
https://doi.org/10.1007/978-3-030-37490-7_2

longer dependent on your parents. You are acting on your dream to visit Africa in response to your college friend's many stories about the continent of Africa and to attend the wedding.

You arrive in Ghana a week before the wedding event and plan to leave one week after the wedding to enable you to see the sights and experience the culture. You are excited on arrival in Ghana not only because of the warmth of the welcome, right from the immigration officials, to the waiting throngs of strangers outside the airport but also because the airport seems quite new and modern. You hear whispers while on the plane that the airport, named "Terminal 3" after Dubai's International Airport Terminal with an identical name, was finished and open for business barely two years ago as a response to increasing travel to Ghana and as part of the government's plan to take advantage of tourist interest in Ghana to make Ghana the main hub for travel to the entire West African region.

You are also excited to be in Ghana because your old college roommate while being one of the warmest, most sociable people you know, is also among the very last ones of your college graduation cohort to get married and you cannot wait to tease him for finally taking a bride.

Your college roommate was always very positive about his country and seemed to genuinely miss his country, especially the food while in college, so naturally you want to experience the food as well. Given his nostalgia about Ghana, his country of origin, it came as no surprise to you when after earning a doctorate and teaching in the USA for a while, your roommate emigrated to Ghana to teach at one of the country's premier universities.

During conversations with your roommate while in college, he spoke passionately about the warmth of Ghana's people, the love of community and ceremony, a deep regard for elderly people and the concept of age and a deep love and respect of the culture and traditions of the elders.

Your roommate did, however, also complain about some of what he considered to be the not-so-positive behaviors and practices of Ghanaians including an inability to keep time and difficulties with discipline in general. Yet, you are quite unprepared for the culture shock you are experiencing since your arrival only a few days ago.

The people are several times warmer than you anticipated, the food is great and because you usually get it hot you are in no danger of contracting food-borne diseases. As a tall, confident Caucasian male who is outgoing and not shy at all, you draw more than just a little interest as people typically greet you with smiles and call you "Obroni." Children are especially interested in talking to you and try to teach you to speak in Twi, the local language. You try your best to learn and speak some words in Twi which draws even more admiration from people that you meet.

Despite the positive experiences, you are quite unprepared for the not-so-positive experiences you have encountered in the short time you have been in Ghana. Your accommodation is close to your roommate's house which is in a suburb of Accra, the capital, about 30-minute drive without traffic and easily more than one hour on a typical day with traffic. On a day with severe traffic, the journey can take two hours and take a toll on both the driver and the passengers.

You immediately notice that the suburb you are currently living in Accra is unlike any suburb in America, Canada, Australia, Europe or Japan. The suburb appears to lack any form of pre-planning as houses are situated haphazardly with dirt roads meandering through them. Sometimes several houses emerge to end the road.

Unlike the typical suburb in the developed world, there are no well-planned and tarred tree-lined roads and there seem to be no zoning rules that guide the siting of houses. Of course, the zoning rules may exist, but even if they do, they are not enforced.

The absence, or lack of enforcement, of zoning rules and of other relevant regulations such as housing permits for construction has resulted in houses that are built without following a pre-determined order. Even worse, there seems to be no system to ensure proper drainage or provide effective services such as waste disposal services, toilets and clean water. Some houses are however self-sufficient in providing these services on their premises including using manholes for toilets and to dispose of wastewater, and drilling bore holes and harvesting rainfall for water.

Even though electricity is provided almost universally from the national grid, some houses are close to energy-independent; using a combination of solar panels and diesel-fueled generator power for electricity when there is lack of supply form the national power pride.

Your curiosity about the siting of buildings in the middle of roads, or what seems to be clearly in the areas set aside for roads or in the path of natural waterways push you to pose a few questions to the locals and to enquire why such a negative practice as building in waterways should be allowed to persist given the consequences for flooding. You had read over the years that flooding was a seasonal and dangerous problem in Ghana which killed several people and destroyed property each year. The situation of homes in public roads also leads to severe problems in moving around and makes transportation of goods extremely difficult.

You are then informed that in Ghana, land is vested, not in the hands of government but rather in the hands of the local people, especially in the hands of the chiefs and family heads. These chiefs and family heads often sell land indiscriminately on the blind side of the families and city-folk and pocket the money. This means the sale of land and siting of houses is often arbitrary and lacks proper planning.

Further, when new settlements begin in the form of suburbs near the capital, they often occur in the context of village settlements near the capital who sell their lands to settlers from the city. Police presence is notoriously absent in Ghanaian villages because the police resist postings to those areas and most probably also because police capacity in the form of buildings, cars and equipment is limited. Consequently, the suburbs usually develop outside of law enforcement.

These suburbs evolve on their own as the land is often indiscriminately sold by village chiefs and family elders. Sometimes surveyors are brought in to help with the siting of roads and to prevent building in waterways. However, anxious potential homeowners and property developers bribe these surveyors to look the other way while they build in the unauthorized locations.

These aggressive property developers and landowners quickly complete their buildings hoping to take advantage of Ghana's negligence laws that make it difficult to pull down buildings or reclaim land once a building has been constructed to the "Lentil" level.

These landowners often cut costs by refusing to employ architects, engineers or landscaping professionals and instead directly employ artisans like masons, carpenters and other artisans who despite their practical skills and context-specific local knowledge are often not educated or at most have received the most basic level of education such as primary education.

Despite their impressive sizes, the buildings in these suburbs themselves often have no building permits, do not typically abide by construction protocols for structural integrity, which is especially important if the buildings have several floors, and do not have draft plan although a formal draft plan is supposed to be kept with the city council.

Further probing reveals that majority of the commercial and residential buildings, especially in the villages near the suburbs, and sometimes even in the houses for rent in the suburbs, do not have functioning toilet facilities. There is no plan for dealing with trash or wastewater as drains are absent and there is no trash-collecting service.

There also seems to be a disregard for the rule of law in the conduct of the renting of houses. Ghana does have a rent control law and a rent control office, and the law stipulates that homeowners must not charge rent for more than six months in advance. However, the risk-reducing cultural practice of charging rent up to several years in advance (one, two, five or ten years in advance) persists. Property owners do not carry out routine maintenance because houses are often rented without proper lease agreements, because no contract is signed and because the homeowners usually disengage from the houses they rent once they take the money until the lease is up.

Surprised by what you are witnessing, you observe the difference between your conceived notions of what you might find in Ghana and the reality. You also notice that the area you are in is not necessarily poor.

Ghana has much poorer areas in the form of slums in the cities and in the rural areas than the suburbs. There are also a few well-organized communities on par with the first world such as Trasacco Valley, Airport Residential area and Cantonments. You are told some of the planned areas were former state housing projects that were well planned and sold to the public.

However, it is the areas that emerged on their own and not part of the few state housing projects, such as the suburb you live in that lack planning. Some of the houses in the suburbs in which you are living are huge, with large compounds and typically bigger than the average houses in your home country in the developed world. They are also structurally made of solid concrete instead of the cheaper wood and plaster you are used to as construction material in your hometown.

There are several cars parked in each of the houses, and each of the houses seems to have domestic helpers, which is again different from the Western world. You learn that despite the shiny and new appearance of the cars, they are not new but rather refurbished accident cars that have been declared condemned and of zero blue book value typically in the USA and other Western countries. However, Ghana's exceptional car restoration industries repairs and restores these cars and sells them for steep prices.

You are stunned by the difference between your expectation and the reality and you ask yourself what the reasons are for the state of things? Clearly, the quality of governance in Ghana may not be as high as governance in Western Europe, America, Canada or Australia, and that is not a surprise given that Ghana has had a functioning democracy for only about 20 years.

However, the interesting question is why have those Ghanaians living in the suburbs chosen the short-sighted option of avoiding all notions of long-term planning and maintenance? Why are they not practicing sanitary disposal of waste? Why have they not invested in proper drainage and effective toilet facilities or compelled their government to do so? Why are they so tolerant of Ghanaian governments that have been accused of corruption and milking of the public purse for their private gain and the neglect of public infrastructure like roads, drainage systems and the provision of basic utilities for so long?

This is especially perplexing because the available drainage systems are often choked with debris and retain filthy wastewater which serves as a breeding ground for mosquitoes. When it rains, the lack of drains and the choked nature of the available drains result in extensive flooding that typically erode away the roads, undermine the structural integrity of buildings and lead to the kind of severe flooding that sometimes carry away cars in traffic. These facts are even more surprising because of the rather high educational levels of some, though not all, of those living there. The residents obviously know that lack of drainage facilities, poor disposal habits and lack of toilet facilities will compromise their health.

Of course, you are aware that Ghana or Africa is not the only region with sanitation problems, but further checks reveal Ghana is ranked one of the dirtiest countries in Africa and is almost at the top when it comes to lack of access to toilets. These problems are clearly self-inflicted and short of seeming judgmental, you make a mental note that it may be cultural.

You ponder further the indiscipline on the roads, with both cars and humans sharing the major streets, with pedestrians indiscriminately crossing busy highways and choosing to avoid designated zebra crossings and constructed foot bridges, and with drivers over-speeding and refusing to obey simple driving laws but with police more interested in collecting bribes from drivers than with keeping the order.

Clearly this is a recipe for disaster. In fact, there is a high rate of accidents between cars and more often between cars and pedestrians on the roads linking the suburb to the city center as pedestrians routinely get hit by cars, sometimes fatally.

You ponder the blatant disregard of the law in almost everything from hawkers selling in the middle of busy streets, street vendors siting kiosks too close to roads, builders disregarding building safety laws and zoning laws during construction and homeowners not bothering to secure housing permits.

Conversations with your friend throws some light on the situation and explains to some extent why these things happen but not how to solve the problems. According to him, the confusing state of the siting of houses and the lack of roads arises from the fact that land tenure is problematic in Ghana and becomes an issue when new suburbs develop.

Land is vested in the custody of the chiefs and family heads, yet citizens are required to register these lands when they acquire them. These chiefs and family heads often sell the land to multiple owners and refuse to do due diligence in terms of siting of roads and drainage facilities. Worse still both the lands commission, and the police have also been cited as among the most corrupt institutions in the country because the officials over time have colluded with these chiefs to sell lands that are designated to be roads or other public facilities.

Your friend further explains that some of the breakdown in the rule of law comes from the fact that the police not only has limited capacity but is often accused of being engaged in corrupt acts even where the capacity to uphold the law exists. Ghana has a large informal sector economy which has almost no police presence both in the rural areas and in the suburbs and inner-city slums.

Research your friend has read suggests that even in the areas where police presence is strong, senior police officers may be involved in the corrupt practices because of a desire to get rich quickly. As a result, it is likely the corruption of junior officers is often overlooked since the junior offices share their spoils with the seniors.

The Ghanaian newspapers have endless stories of police corruption and there are even videos of police engaged in police corruption posted on the internet. Several international surveys including the Afro-barometer survey identify the police as among the most corrupt organizations in Ghana.

However, not all the problems are from weak law enforcement. According to your friend, Ghana was under military dictatorship for more than 20 years, and during those times, the country was poorer, but discipline was effected by a no-nonsense military regime under the leadership of Flight Lieutenant Jerry John Rawlings. The streets of Ghana during that era were clean, citizens did not dare flout the law and citizens that could not afford water-closet toilets and septic tanks had pit latrines or pan latrines which they had to pay professional night stool carriers to regularly empty.

However, the transition to democracy brought with it significant rural-urban migration and a true sense of freedom not only to be free of oppression but to be free to flout every single law possible. It was the opening of this proverbial "Pandora's box" that led to a culture of apathy or laissez faire that is costing the nation dear. Ghanaians have developed this "enye hwee" attitude which is Twi and translates to mean "it does not matter" as a response to all incorrect action and as a call to forgive incorrect, wrongful and unlawful action in the name of keeping the peace.

It is precisely this "enye hwee" attitude that is probably behind Ghana's stellar record of public peace, tolerance, community and friendliness. However, it may also be the reason behind the very tolerant attitude toward political and police corruption, indiscipline in construction and on the roads, hawking on major streets, indiscriminate disposal of plastic waste, and the siting of houses in the middle of designated roads and in the path of natural waterways.

According to your friend, it is just impossible to have enough police to monitor all the citizens so it is actually the discipline of the citizens and their desire to do the right thing is what will regulate behavior such as depositing the trash in the roads and the available drains, and the indiscriminate throwing of toilet in black plastic bags on roads or on to neighbors' yards (a practice called "shit bombing").

How can Ghana overcome these self-inflicted problems including corruption, indiscipline and a blatant disregard for the law that has such negative long-term consequences for its growth? How can the nation transform this "enye hwee" culture to serve only good causes?

Your thoughts switch back to the present situation. Your roommate's wedding day draws near, and you are in for another surprise. Ghanaians have two weddings instead of one: "a traditional marriage" and "a formal marriage." This means Ghanaians men marry their wives two times.

The Western notion of engagement has been transformed into the Ghanaian traditional marriage. This is followed by the formal wedding which mirrors the church wedding in the Western world. It is often held in the church or a law court but sometimes in an event center, a conference hall, a hotel or a resort. This formal ceremony is often accompanied by the signing of legal documents and is recognized by law.

The traditional marriage, at least among the coast-dwelling Fantes, involves many steps. The prospective wife must be introduced to the family of the groom and the groom must be introduced to the family of the prospective wife. The groom then follows up with another visit in the company of his aunts and uncles to collect "a list" of items that he must purchase for the bride-to-be to support her in her new role as a wife.

These include traveling bags, ladies' handbags, ladies make-up kit, traditional cloth such as traditional Kente, Dumas and other cloths produced by Ghanaian textile companies, panties, brassieres, slippers, cooking utensils, plates, bowls, cups and so on. The man must also provide three rings for the wedding; one of the rings is for the bridegroom and the other two (the engagement ring and the wedding ring) are for the bride. The list of purchases is independent of the expense of the traditional wedding itself, which involves the provision of food for guests and payment for entertainment.

Clearly the wedding itself is also expensive. Usually, there is the need to rent hotel rooms so the bridegroom will be away from distractions. The groom typically has groomsmen who wear matching outfits on the day and must be housed for the period of the wedding. The groom typically bears the cost of this. The groom must ensure the wedding is the talk of town and is a day the wife will never forget.

The bride also has bridesmaids that must be dressed and accommodated. The bridal gown, the hotel rooms for the bride and the bridal party, the cost of the wedding ceremony itself, and even more importantly the cost of the typically elaborate wedding reception and the honeymoon are all astronomical.

However, these are culturally and socially expected despite low incomes in a relatively poor country. These expectations reflect values that may be cultural in origin and cannot be managed without education and effective leadership.

Clearly Ghanaians spend a lot on weddings and funerals. They also spend a lot on naming ceremonies and church functions such as "harvests" where the Church gives thanks to God.

As a Ghanaian who has been to different churches all my life, it is safe to say that Ghanaians, at least rural Ghanaians and a large portion of city-dwellers, spend more on these types of ceremonies: funerals (deaths), weddings (marriage), Church harvests and naming ceremonies (births) than they spend on productive investments such as building a house or educating their children consistent with Banerjee and Dufflo's (2007) account of the economic lives of the poor.

This is clearly a self-inflicted problem that does not bode well for Ghana's future. The pertinent question though is why? Why spend so much on ceremonies instead of investment? Why these self-inflicted problems including over-spending on ceremonies like weddings and funerals. Why the corruption, indiscipline and a blatant disregard for the law that has such negative long-term consequences for its growth?

Discussing possible strategies to answers to these questions is the purpose of this book. Clearly the problems facing Ghana are multifaceted and complex and include both internal and external factors some of which are contemporary and others historical. Some are cultural but the solution to all it seems must start with a change in mindsets. A change in mindsets can only come with effective education.

Ghana has historically suffered from the negative effects of slavery (which robbed it of its able citizens and set tribes against each other), colonization (which depleted resources like gold, diamond, bauxite, manganese, cobalt and zinc and programmed the mind of the colonized to feel inferior and incapable of original thinking and innovation) and an unjust world economic order (that has frozen it out of capital markets ostentatiously because of weak institutions). Like other African countries, access to credit is difficult for Ghanaians. They do not have access to credit cards and pay high interest for loans. The assets they have like land and houses cannot be used as collateral because they are not properly documented, and the property rights are probably not secure. This kind of capital is in the words of De Soto (2000) "Dead Capital." Ghana needs to document these assets to "raise its capital from the dead" to finance productive investment.

Ghana also has severe institutional problems because the transition from military rule to democracy was not without cost (Armah 2016). Flight Lt. Rawlings and the Provincial National Defense Council (PNDC), the military rulers in power that oversaw the transition to democracy, probably had incentives to ensure that there were enough loopholes in the constitution to arrogate almost all power to the civilian ruler that followed the military because they were handing over power to themselves. Flight Lt. Rawlings, the same military ruler took over the reins of the subsequent democracy that was established as the head of the PNDC that had then been re-named the National Democratic Congress (NDC).

In particular, the president under the new 1992 constitution has sweeping powers that enables him to appoint the heads and board members of all public and semi-public institutions including the boards of public utilities, universities, agricultural marketing boards, the police and all security services, and health institutions (Armah 2016).

This is particularly telling as Ghana was initially a socialist country and so the economic life is not dominated by private enterprise as in Western countries and rather leaves significant control of its economic life in the hands of government.

A democratic country which arrogates significant power to its executives is bound to have poor institutions especially if it runs a "winner takes all system" of government and the cultural check on corruption is not only weak but there is also cultural tolerance of corruption. Furthermore, from what you have learned so far from your friend and from the local people, the rule of law is weak and land tenure is ineffective and property rights are weak.

However, you realize that the problems Ghana faces are more than institutional problems and they are more than the problems generated by external factors. It is true that Ghana is plagued by several externally inflicted problems such as a history filled with negative occurrences like colonization, the slave trade and an unjust world economic order where developed countries subsidize their producers and force developing countries like Ghana to open up their markets leading to dumping of cheaper goods into Ghana that kills Ghanaian businesses.

However, it seems that majority of the problems also seem cultural and self-inflicted and may at least in part, something to do with what Huntington described as a lack of appreciation for the values of "*hard work, thrift, discipline, and organization.*"

It is not strange that people with a lower level of income tend to take shortcuts when it comes in respect of quality specifications and safety features. However, there is also evidence that at least one or two poorer African countries, for example, Rwanda, seem to be more disciplined. They have cleaner cities and suburbs, possess functioning toilets and better laid-out roads and waste disposal services and so suffer less from drainage and flooding problems and so deal with less filth and stench than Ghanaians do.

On the other hand, there are several African countries in Ghana's situation, including large countries like Nigeria and Kenya all of which have transitioned from military rule to functioning democracies, so the problem remains an interesting one.

Why the deplorable situations in the new suburbs springing up around the capital of Ghana but which is not unique to Ghana? Even if such suburbs are neither extremely poor nor are their slums poor why the "laissez faire attitude"? Ghanaians like to say "enye hwee" meaning "its ok or it does not matter" to anything that is incorrect, wrong or imperfect as a means of keeping the peace and avoiding conflict but it is this very "enye hwee" philosophy that is breeding the kind of mediocrity, inefficiency and indiscipline that reduces the quality of life of Ghanaians.

Given Ghana's diversified sources of income including oil, gold (top exporter in Africa), cocoa (top quality producer and second largest producer in the world), tuna (second largest producer in Africa) and tourism, Ghana should be far from poor. Ghanaian suburbs should be able to benefit from well-planned houses, clean streets, effective drainage and toilet systems just like a fellow African country like Rwanda which does not even have these same resources.

However, if Ghana does not abandon the "enye hwee" mantra and chooses to overlook or forgive all acts of corruption, indiscipline, ineptitude and laziness, this can develop into a dangerous culture that will hold back the country's development.

I next look at the literature on the culture, institutions and development and the inter-relationships between them. I do this to try to understand the cultural and institutional basis of some of the blatant self-inflicted problems we have identified in the story above in order to discuss possible solutions to turn things around. I finish this chapter by reproducing this quote from Tabellini (2007), which seems to capture the essence of the story captured in this chapter:

> Economic backwardness is typically associated with a large range of institutional, organizational and government failures, along many dimensions. In several poor or stagnating countries, politicians are ineffective and corrupt, public goods are under-provided and public policies confer rents to privileged élites, law enforcement is inadequate, moral hazard is widespread inside public and private organizations. There is not just one institutional failure. Typically, the countries or regions that fail in one dimension also fail in many other aspects of collective behavior. (Tabellini 2007)

I acknowledge that institutional economics championed by among others North (1990) and Acemoglu, Johnson and Robinson (2001) has convinced the economics world that developmental challenges are mainly due to institutional problems. In particular Lopez-Claros and Perotti (2014) explain that these institutional problems have to do with a historical occurrence of despotic rule. This likely applies to Ghana that transitioned from a military dictatorship to democratic rule in 1992 after almost two decades of despotic military rule under flight benign dictator Flight Lt. Rawlings.

However, it is not clear that historically weak institutions where all power was allocated to a despotic leader can explain away all of Ghana's developmental challenges. Even though governance is key, in the case of Ghana it seems the people themselves, their culture, beliefs and how their minds are programmed cannot be ignored in understanding developmental challenges.

Bibliography

Acemoglu, D., Johnson, S., & Robinson, J. A. (2001). The Colonial Origins of Comparative Development: An Empirical Investigation. *American Economic Review, 91*(5), 1369–1401.

Armah, S. E. (2016). Strategies to Stimulate Ghana's Economic Transformation and Diversification. *Ashesi Economics Lecture Series Journal, 2*(1), 9–16.

Banerjee, A. V., & Duflo, E. (2007). The Economic Lives of the Poor. *The Journal of Economic Perspectives, 21*(1), 141–167.

De Soto, H. (2000). *The Mystery of Capital: Why Capitalism Triumphs in the West and Fails Everywhere Else.* New York: Basic Books.

Lopez-Claros, A., & Perotti, V. (2014). *Does Culture Matter for Development?* Policy Research Working Paper No. WPS 7092. Washington, DC: World Bank Group.

North, D. (1990). *Institutions, Institutional Change, and Economic Performance.* New York: Cambridge University Press.

Tabellini, G. (2007). *Institutions and Culture.* (IGIR working paper 330). Milan, Italy: University of Bocconi.

CHAPTER 3

A Review of the Culture: Institutions Nexus

Abstract This chapter compares different definitions of institutions and culture and illustrates how culture and institutions are inter-related and interconnected in their effect or impacts on development. The chapter also highlights why conventional, textbook, neoclassical prescriptions for Africa's problems such as increasing saving rates and Washington Consensus-based solutions such as liberalization of the economy and divestiture of state properties have not delivered on the prosperity promised to Africans although they seemed reasonable solutions ex ante. These kinds of prescriptions typically ignore the cultural context and hardly ever focus on strengthening institutions in ways that are culturally sensitive.

Keywords Culture • Washington consensus • Institutions and development

The story about Ghana from Chap. 2, though fictional, is meant to illustrate to the reader the significant challenges of African development by focusing on Ghana, which is considered a mild case of African underdevelopment. Hopefully the reader was adequately exposed to the reality and enormity of the problem.

In particular, the challenge of African development is not a challenge of resources because African countries like Ghana have plenty of resources. In fact,

Sachs and Warner (2001) have argued that plentiful resources can lead to a curse instead of a blessing.

It is how the resources are used, which is in turn a reflection of how the people "think," how they "make decisions" and what they "believe in that is the crux of the development challenge." Hofstede (2001) defined culture as the "programming of the mind," and I hope the story illustrated what he meant.

Why will a group of people waste resources to build houses and not plan for roads and waterways so that their buildings always get flooded and they cannot move around when it rains? Why will a group of people devote all their resources to build a place of worship and to line the pockets of the religious leader with wealth while they have no money to build good roads or drains? Are their minds programmed to make that choice and who programmed their minds to make that choice?

I also wanted to use the story to convey why conventional, textbook, neoclassical prescriptions for Africa's problems such as (i) increasing saving rates or reducing population rates, and (ii) Washington Consensus-based solutions such as liberalization of the economy and divestiture of state properties have not worked to a great extent for Africa although they seemed reasonable solutions ex ante.

Some authors have claimed none of Africa's development challenges are self-inflicted and that external factors are fully responsible for Africa's problems (Rodney 1981; Jarrett 1996). Others, such as Huntington and Harrison (2000) (in the case of Ghana), as well as Rostow (1960) and Bauer (1972) argued that African culture is antithetical to development.

I do not intend to overlook the difficulties that the external environment presents to Africans in general, and to Ghana in particular, because it did put Africa, and Ghana to be specific, at a disadvantage. For example, slavery robbed Ghana of its most valuable human capital and colonization undermined the self-confidence of the Ghanaian and robbed Ghana of all its major resources: gold, diamonds, cobalt, bauxite as well as income from cash crops such as cocoa, coffee and rubber. There is also an unjust world economic order at play where importer oligopsony power undermine and lower the prices of African exports such as cocoa and coffee over time keeping such countries in debt. I understand this.

In fact, some passionate Pan Africanists such as Kwame Nkrumah, Ghana's first president (see Nkrumah 1961, "I Speak of Freedom") argued so many years ago that Western solutions will not work for Africa.

Nkrumah insisted that only Africans can help Africa and urged Africans to form the "United States of Africa" to counter Western influence because the Western world was working against Africa and not helping Africa. Nkrumah went as far as to define the term "neocolonialism" to describe the frustrations he felt toward what he perceived as Western undermining of African development efforts. Africa's problems, according to Nkrumah, demanded African or home-grown or internally generated solutions.

I concur with Nkrumah that Africa's solutions should come from Africa. I will, however, not go so far as to condemn well-meaning Western development economists and Western philanthropists who genuinely wanted to bring a positive change to Africa.

I do agree with Nkrumah that conventional neoclassical, economic solutions failed in Africa because they are difficult to implement and probably were impotent even when effected because the traditional culture and institutions of the African people were inconsistent with these textbook-based, neoclassical prescriptions and in any case, African cuture were largely ignored in the designing and implementations of solutions.

Even more telling, the African culture and belief systems remained largely unchanged after implementation of the Western prescriptions because the implementation of these strategies ignored the African indigenous population who were never engaged in implementing these solutions.

I argue that, given how attached Africans are to their culture, it may be time to re-focus on the role of culture in the development process in tackling African development. Although this may sound ironic coming from a USA-trained economist like myself, my ten years in Ghana after fifteen years of academic training and professional work experience in the USA has exposed me enough to Africa to warrant my stand.

Interestingly, cultural economics or the economics of how culture affects economic outcomes is enjoying a re-birth worldwide in the formal development economics literature in the twenty-first century as development scholars now seem to agree that culture matters in charting the developmental progress for developing nations (Grief 1994; Granato et al. 1996; Serageldin and Tabaroff 1992; Clague et al. 2001; Odhiambo 2002; Guiso et al. 2006; Tabellini 2008; Alesina and Giuliano 2015, and Klitgaard 2017).

For example, according to Heffner (2002), Huntington's (2000) seminal research led him to conclude that "culture matters in development" and in answer to how much culture matters Landes (2000) published his famous book aptly titled *Culture Makes All the Difference*.

In contrast to the difficulties cultural economics faced in getting universal acceptance, institutional economics, championed by among others, Douglas North (who won a Nobel Prize for his work), and the research trio of Daron Acemoglu, James Robinson and Simon Johnson has more easily received universal acceptance. The quality and effectiveness of economic and political institutions is now recognized by economists as the main determinant of growth (Acemoglu et al. 2001; Hall and Jones 1999; Durlauf 2018).

Effective, inclusive political and economic institutions are now regarded as pertinent for growth and development, at least in the African context, in addition to Solow (1956s) summary of neoclassical growth determinants such as capital/labor ratios, saving rates and population growth rates because of the poor state of institutions in African countries, Ghana not excluded.

I argue, as do Huntington (2000) and Landes (2000), that the cultural context is especially poignant in determining development in Africa and is one that cannot and should not be ignored in the African context.

Not so long ago, however, economists were not interested in considering culture as a viable determinant of economic growth and development because of a myriad of problems (Granato et al. 1996; Guiso et al. 2006). I am not trying to argue that culture suddenly became of interest to economists in the twenty-first century, far from that. Rather, culture has enjoyed sporadic attention from economists over time and is back again in vogue in the present time.

According to Njoh (2006), some development economists (e.g., Rostow 1960; Bauer 1972) had argued in the past that African culture is antithetical to development. Banfield (1958) argued that there are aspects of culture that are growth inhibiting and must be changed in order to enhance development. Other economists indiscriminately endorsed all aspects of African culture and traditional practices as promoting of development (e.g., Rodney 1981; Jarrett 1996).

The hands-off attitude economists developed toward culture until quite recently can be attributed to several reasons but key among those reasons were:

(i) The difficulty in defining culture given its extremely broad scope and multi-dimensional nature (Alesina and Giuliano 2015; Guiso et al. 2008; Akpomuvie 2010; Tabellini 2008).

(ii) The difficulty in measuring culture or even establishing cultural variables and keeping data on cultural variables (Roland 2016; Granato et al. 1996).
(iii) The problems involved in disentangling the effects of culture on development from the effects of institutions on development since the two concepts are notoriously difficult to differentiate and are for all intents and purposes, simultaneously determined or endogenous (Alesina and Giuliano 2015).

To expand on the problem of interconnections between institutions and culture, recall that institutions can influence culture and institutions can also be influenced by culture in determining development. Evidence of the impact of culture on institutions (Fisman and Miguel 2007) and the effect of institutions on culture (Putnam 1993) both exist. Culture and institutions are endogenous variables so the decomposition of their effects on development often proves difficult.

(iv) The problem of double causality between development and growth on one hand and culture on the other hand has been documented. Development has been shown to affect culture according to modernization theory (Inglehart and Baker 2000) apart from the claims that culture affects growth and development (Gorodnichenko and Roland 2017; Greif 1994, 2006a, b; Bisin and Verdier 2000, 2001; Doepke and Zilibotti 2008; Fernández et al. 2004; Fernández and Fogli 2009; Giuliano 2007; Barro and McCleary 2003; Knack and Keefer 1997; Hall and Jones 1999).

In this book, development is considered to involve not only an ability of people to have sustenance self-esteem and freedom (Todaro and Smith 2006) but also involves such factors as education, growth, health, unemployment, inequality and poverty so that a "developed country" must have healthy people who enjoy good governance under effective, non-corrupted leadership, have access to sustenance (food, shelter, water, clothing), self-esteem, freedom of choice as well as high levels of education and income and low levels of poverty, unemployment and inequality.

To illustrate the effect of income on culture, consider, for example, the demographic transition concept, where a culture of fewer births displaces a culture of numerous offspring as people get wealthier (Todaro and Smith 2006).

To illustrate the effect of educational levels on culture, see the literature on women's participation in the labor force where, as the general level of education of the populace increases, more women get educated, yielding a more educated work force (Fernández 2013; Todaro and Smith 2006).

To illustrate the effect of leadership on culture, see, for example, the role of President Paul Kagame in helping to turn around the fortunes of Rwanda after the 1996 genocide by transforming the culture in Rwanda into a pro-market pro-growth one. Lee Kwan Yew who also transformed the economy and culture of Singapore from a third world one to a first world one (Yew 2000).

(v) Finally, culture is dynamic (although slow moving) and apart from its inter-dependence on institutions also can be influenced by among other factors, income and educational levels, leadership and technology.

The above discussions indicate that given the dynamic nature of culture, identifying a significant effect of culture on development (negative or positive) may be transient since intermediate effects of other variables on culture, such as institutions and education, may change with time and may even change signs in terms of effect.

However, this does not mean re-enforcing and self-sustaining, positive or negative effects of culture on development, despite the intermediate effects are ruled out. Even more complex is the fact that there may be two-way relationship between culture and development. Not only does culture determine development but different levels of development illicit different cultural practices and beliefs.

In the rest of the chapter, I briefly summarize and compare the different definitions of culture and institutions and development as described in the literature. Next, I discuss the themes identified in the literature on the effects of culture. I then briefly summarize the literature conclusions on the inter-relationships between culture, institutions and development. I do this to substantiate the point that culture matters in the development context and may make a lot of difference in the African context despite long neglect of the subject in the economics literature.

Definitions of Culture

Growing up as a young man in Ghana, I was made to understand that culture referred to the "way of life" of a people including their "beliefs, religion, norms, conventions, artifacts, song, music, dance and performance." Although I do not quite recall where I got this definition, formal definitions of culture in the literature on cultural economics do not seem radically different from this simple definition.

According to Roland (2016), "Culture is the set of values and beliefs people have about how the world (both nature and society) works as well as the norms of behavior derived from that set of values" (Roland 2016). In comparison, Hofstede claims, "Culture is the programming of the mind that distinguishes one group of people from another" (Hofstede 1980).

From an empirical perspective, Guiso, Sapienza and Zingales (2006) claim culture refer to "those customary beliefs and values that ethnic, religious, and social groups transmit fairly unchanged from generation to generation" (Guiso et al. 2006). Boyd and Richerson claim culture is defined as the "decision-making heuristics or rules of thumb that have evolved to serve our need to make decisions in complex and uncertain environments" (Boyd and Richerson 1985, 2005).

According to Greif (1994), "Cultural beliefs are the ideas and thoughts common to several people that govern interaction—between these people and among them, their gods, and other groups—and differ from knowledge in that they are not empirically discovered or analytically proved. In general, cultural beliefs become identical and commonly maintained, and communicated" (Greif 1994).

According to Lopez-Claros and Perotti (2014), Murdock (1965) argues that a culture consists of "habits that are shared by members of a society, whether a primitive tribe or an advanced nation. It is the product of learning, not of heredity." "The cultures of the world are systems of collective habits. The differences observable among them are the cumulative product of mass learning under diverse geographic and social conditions" (Murdock, pp. 113–114).

Andah and Bolarinwa (1994) viewed culture as the sum of values, beliefs, attitudes, customs and pattern of behaviors in a society. They consider these as a vital pillar of social and economic transformation so economic strategies that ignore culture are doomed to fail.

Thus far, cultural economics is quite young, and economics have paid little heed to trying to differentiate between cultural beliefs and cultural values. So far, culture has been used to refer to both beliefs and values. The definitions of culture used so far imply that culture has to do with the "informal part" of the way of life and does not seem to address the formal or "legal" part. Economists have referred to the legal way of life as "institutions." So, in this book, following Alesina and Giuliano (2015), institutions refer to the formal rules that govern the way of life of a people (laws, policies, regulations), while culture refers to the informal rules (norms, beliefs, conventions, values, religion).

Definitions of Institutions

North (1990) defines institutions as "the humanly devised constraints that structure human interactions." They are made up of formal constraints (rules, laws, constitutions), informal constraints (norms of behavior, convention, and self-imposed codes of conduct), and their enforcement characteristics.

Defined this way, culture is a subset of institutions. To distinguish between culture and institutions, we follow Alesina and Giuliano (2015), as the literature has done, and define culture as "informal institutions" and formal institutions as simply "institutions" (Alesina and Giuliano 2015).

North's (1990) definition assign formal constraints to the government (laws, rules, constitutions) and informal constraints (norms of behavior, convention and self-imposed codes of conduct) are part of the heritage called culture.

Acemoglu, Johnson and Robinson (2006) define institutions as "mechanisms through which social choices are determined and implemented" they distinguish between economic institutions and political institutions. Political institutions are mechanisms for the distribution of political power across different socioeconomic groups. Political power, in turn, determines economic institutions (Acemoglu et al. 2006).

Greif (2006b) defines an institution as "a system of social factors that conjointly generates a regularity of behavior." "Social factors," means "man-made, nonphysical factors that are exogenous to each person they influence," including "rules, beliefs, norms, and organizations" (Greif 2006b).

North (1990, p. 3) provides the classic definition of institutions as "the rules of the game in a society" or, more formally, "humanly devised constraints that shape interaction." In consequence, "they structure incentives in human exchange, whether, political, social, or economic."

By way of comparison, Greif (2006a, b, p. 39) states that institutions constitute "a system of rules, beliefs, and norms, and organizations that together generate a regularity of (social) behavior" (italics removed).

Baland, Bourguignon, Platteau and Verdier describe institutions as "rules, procedures, or other human devices that constrain individual behavior, with a view to making individual expectations about others' behavior converge and to allowing individual actions to become more coordinated."

Rodrik (2005) provides examples of what institutions are by focusing on property rights. He divides institutions into those that are (i) market creating (e.g., property rights) (ii) market regulating (rules for addressing market failures) (iii) market-stabilizing (macro-level monetary fiscal and financial policies) and (iv) market-legitimizing (political inclusiveness via democratic rules and social insurance).

The myriad of definitions of culture and institutions hopefully gave the reader some insights into the similarities and differences between these two concepts as treated by the literature. We next examine themes that have evolved in cultural economics literature.

Themes in Cultural Economics and the Relationships with Development

The Inertia of Culture: Culture Is Slow Moving

The reason for culture being slow moving is that cultural transmission is mostly vertical and takes place between parents and children. There is a horizontal component to cultural transmission, based on peers, but it generally plays a much smaller role. Cultural inertia is now well-documented (Roland 2016; Durlauf 2018).

Cultural inertia has important implications. A first one is that culture may be a fundamental determinant of institutions. This is because while institutions can change rather suddenly, culture changes very rarely, and takes time to be established. Once a culture is established, it takes a lot of time to change so culture can determine institutions and though institutions can also change culture this may take more time.

Trust as a Key Cultural Variable

According to Roland (2016), trust is by far the most researched of the different cultural variables. Trust has been interpreted in various ways: culture of cooperation (related to social capital), culture of active political participation, generalized morality (as opposed to morality limited to one's ingroup, etc.). Societies with more trust have been found to be associated with higher income per capita, innovation, and financial market development. As Arrow's (1972) quote below shows, Huntington's (2000) claim that trust matters for the development of African countries like Ghana is not misplaced:

> Virtually every commercial transaction has within itself an element of trust, certainly any transaction conducted over a time. It can be plausibly argued that much of the economic backwardness in the world can be explained by the lack of mutual confidence. (Arrow 1972)

The idea that generalized trust and generalized morality lead to better collective outcomes has a long history in other social sciences (Banfield 1958; Gambetta 1988; Putnam 1993; Fukuyama 1995; Coleman 1990).

Landes (1998), BeNer and Putterman (1998) and Platteau (2000) emphasize the relevance of culture and morality to economic development and to the functioning of institutions. In cross-country data, generalized trust has been shown to be correlated with favorable economic outcomes (Knack and Keefer 1997) and with indicators of good government (La Porta et al. 1997).

Individualism Versus Collectivism

Another often researched cultural variable is the individualism-collectivism variable due to Dutch sociologist Hofstede (Greif 1994; Gorodnichenko and Roland 2011; Roland 2016). Individualistic societies are associated with high earnings and achievement while collective societies are not.

There is also a literature based on the work of cross-cultural psychologist Shalom Schwartz (1999), which is closely related to the individualism-collectivism variable identified by Hofstede. Tabellini (2010) provide a historically compelling analysis of cultural divergence between China and Europe using the individualism versus collectivism variable due to sociologist Hofstede. They explains why, historically, a culture of collectivism held back China for so long while a culture of individualism spurred Europe to great economic achievements. For brevity we will not analyze the remaining dimensions of Hofstede's cultural variables. Interested readers should see Husted (1999), Bontis and Seleim (2009), Taras et al. (2010) and Lanier and Kirshner (2018).

BIBLIOGRAPHY

Acemoglu, D., Johnson, S., & Robinson, J. A. (2001). The Colonial Origins of Comparative Development: An Empirical Investigation. *American Economic Review, 91*(5), 1369–1401.

Acemoglu, D., Johnson, S., & Robinson, J. A. (2006, December). The Colonial Origins of Comparative Development: An Empirical Investigation. *American Economic Review, 91*, 1369–1401.

Akpomuvie, O. B. (2010). Culture and the Challenges of Development in Africa: Towards A Hybridization of Traditional and Modern Values. *African Research Review, 4*(1), 288–297.

Alesina, A., & Giuliano, P. (2015). Culture and Institutions. *Journal of Economic Literature, 53*(4), 898–944.

Andah, B. W., & Bolarinwa, K. (1994). *A Celebration of Africa's Roots and Legacy*. Ibadan: Fajee Publishers Ltd.

Arrow, K. J. (1972). Gifts and Exchanges. *Philosophy & Public Affairs, 1*, 343–362.

Banfield, E. (1958). *The Moral Basis of a Backward Society*. New York: Simon and Schuster.

Barro, R. J., & McCleary, R. (2003). *Religion and Economic Growth* (No. w9682). National Bureau of Economic Research.

Bauer, P. T. (1972). *Dissent on Development: Studies and Debates in Development Economics*. Cambridge, MA: Harvard University Press.

BeNer, A., & Putterman, L. (1998). Values, Institutions, and Economics. *The Good Society, 8*(2), 14–16.

Bisin, A., & Verdier, T. (2000). "Beyond the Melting Pot": Cultural Transmission, Marriage, and the Evolution of Ethnic and Religious Traits. *The Quarterly Journal of Economics, 115*(3), 955–988.

Bisin, A., & Verdier, T. (2001). The Economics of Cultural Transmission and the Dynamics of Preferences. *Journal of Economic Theory, 97*(2), 298–319.

Bontis, N., & Seleim, A. (2009). The Relationship Between Culture and Corruption: A Cross-National Study. *Journal of Intellectual Capital, 10*(1), 165–184. https://doi.org/10.1108/14691930910922978.

Boyd, R., & Richerson, P. J. (1985). *Culture and the Evolutionary Process*. Chicago: University of Chicago Press.

Boyd, R., & Richerson, P. J. (2005). *The Origin and Evolution of Cultures*. Oxford: Oxford University Press.

Clague, C., Knack, S., & Gleason, S. (2001). Determinants of Lasting Democracy in Poor Countries: Culture, Development, and Institutions. *The Annals of the American Academy of Political and Social Science, 573*(1), 16–41.

Coleman, J. S. (1990). *Foundations of Social Theory*. Cambridge, MA: Harvard University Press.

Doepke, M., & Zilibotti, F. (2008). Occupational Choice and the Spirit of Capitalism. *The Quarterly Journal of Economics, 123*(2), 747–793.

Durlauf, S. (2018). *Institutions, Development and Growth: Where Does Evidence Stand*. Economic Development and Institutions Working Paper 18, 4.

Fernández, R. (2013). Cultural Change as Learning: The Evolution of Female Labor Force Participation over a Century. *American Economic Review, 103*(1), 472–500.

Fernández, R., & Fogli, A. (2009). Culture: An Empirical Investigation of Beliefs, Work, and Fertility. *American Economic Journal: Macroeconomics, 1*(1), 146–177.

Fernández, R., Fogli, A., & Olivetti, C. (2004). Mothers and Sons: Preference Formation and Female Labor Force Dynamics. *The Quarterly Journal of Economics, 119*(4), 1249–1299.

Fisman, R., & Miguel, E. (2007). Corruption, Norms, and Legal Enforcement: Evidence from Diplomatic Parking Tickets. *Journal of Political Economy, 115*(6), 1020–1048.

Fukuyama, F. (1995). *Trust: The Social Virtues and the Creation of Prosperity* (Vol. 99). New York: Free Press.

Gambetta, D. (1988). Fragments of an Economic Theory of the Mafia. *European Journal of Sociology/Archives Européennes de Sociologie, 29*(1), 127–145.

Giuliano, P. (2007). Living Arrangements in Western Europe: Does Cultural Origin Matter? *Journal of the European Economic Association, 5*(5), 927–952.

Gorodnichenko, Y., & Roland, G. (2011). Which Dimensions of Culture Matter for Long-Run Growth? *American Economic Review, 101*(3), 492–498. https://doi.org/10.1257/aer.101.3.492.

Gorodnichenko, Y., & Roland, G. (2017). Culture, Institutions, and the Wealth of Nations. *Review of Economics and Statistics, 99*(3), 402–416.

Granato, J., Inglehart, R., & Leblang, D. (1996). The Effect of Cultural Values on Economic Development: Theory, Hypotheses, and Some Empirical Tests. *American Journal of Political Science, 40*, 607–631.

Greif, A. (1994). Cultural Beliefs and the Organization of Society: A Historical and Theoretical Reflection on Collectivist and Individualist Societies. *Journal of Political Economy, 102*(5), 912–950.

Greif, A. (2006a). Family Structure, Institutions, and Growth: The Origins and Implications of Western Corporations. *American Economic Review, 96*(2), 308–312.

Greif, A. (2006b). *Institutions and the Path to the Modern Economy: Lessons from Medieval Trade*. Cambridge: Cambridge University Press.

Guiso, L., Sapienza, P., & Zingales, L. (2006). Does Culture Affect Economic Outcomes? *Journal of Economic Perspectives, 20*(2), 23–48.

Guiso, L., Sapienza, P., & Zingales, L. (2008). Social Capital as Good Culture. *Journal of the European Economic Association, 6*(2–3), 295–320.

Hall, R. E., & Jones, C. I. (1999). Why Do Some Countries Produce So Much More Output Per Worker Than Others? *The Quarterly Journal of Economics, 114*(1), 83–116.

Heffner, F. (2002). The Role of Beliefs and Cultural Attitudes in Economic Development. *The Review of Regional Studies, 32*(1), 1–8.

Hofstede, G. (1980). *Culture's consequences: International differences in workrelated values*. Beverly Hills: Sage Publishers.

Hofstede, G. (2001). *Culture's Consequences: Comparing Values, Behaviours, Institutions, and Organizations Across Nations* (2nd ed.). Thousand Oaks: Sage.

Huntington, S. (2000). *Political Order in Changing Societies*. New Haven: Yale University Press.

Huntington, S. P., & Harrison, L. E. (2000). *Culture Matters: How Values Shape Human Progress*. New York: Basic Books.

Husted, B. (1999). Corruption and Culture. *Journal of International Business Studies, 30*(2), 339. 2nd Qtr.

Inglehart, R., & Baker, W. E. (2000). Modernization, Cultural Change, and the Persistence of Traditional Values. *American Sociological Review, 65*(1), 19–51.

Jarrett, A. (1996). *The Under-Development of Africa: Colonialism, Neo-Colonialism and Socialism*. Lanham/New York/London: University Press of America.

Klitgaard, R. (2017, June 13). *On Corruption and Culture*. Paper Presented at the Public Integrity and Anti-Corruption Workshop at Nuffield College, Oxford.

Knack, S., & Keefer, P. (1997). Does Social Capital Have an Economic Payoff? A Cross-Country Investigation. *The Quarterly Journal of Economics, 112*(4), 1251–1288.

La Porta, R., Lopez-de-Silanes, F., Shleifer, A., & Vishny, R. W. (1997). Trust in Large Organizations. *American Economic Review Papers and Proceedings, 87*, 333–338.

Landes, D. (1998). *Culture Matters: How Values Shape Human Progress*, L. E. Harrison & Samuel P. Huntington (Eds.), 2000. New York: Basic Books.

Landes, D. (2000). Culture Makes Almost All the Difference. In *Culture Matters: How Values Shape Human Progress* (pp. 2–13). New York: Basic Books.

Lanier, C., & Kirshner, M. (2018). Corruption and Culture: Empirical Analysis of Long-Term Indulgence and Corrupt Systems. *The Review of Business, and Interdisciplinary Journal on Risk and Society, 38*(2), 30–43.

Lopez-Claros, A., & Perotti, V. (2014). *Does Culture Matter for Development?* Policy Research Working Paper No. WPS 7092. Washington, DC: World Bank Group.

Murdock, G. P. (1965). *Culture and Society: Twenty-Four Essays.* Pittsburgh: University of Pittsburgh Press.

Njoh, A. (2006). *Tradition, Culture and Development in Africa Historical Lessons for Modern Development Planning.* London: Routledge.

Nkrumah, K. (1961). *I Speak of Freedom: A Statement of African Ideology.* New York: Praeger.

North, D. (1990). *Institutions, Institutional Change, and Economic Performance.* New York: Cambridge University Press.

Odhiambo, E. S. (2002). The Cultural Dimensions of Development in Africa. *African Studies Review, 45*(3), 1–16.

Platteau, J. P. (2000). Does Africa Need Land Reform? In *Evolving Land Rights, Policy and Tenure in Africa* (pp. 51–74). London: IIED.

Putnam, R. (1993). Explaining Institutional Performance. In *Making Democracy Work* (pp. 83–120). Princeton: Princeton University Press.

Rodney, W. (1981). *How Europe Underdeveloped Africa.* Washington, DC: Howard University Press.

Rodrik, D. (2005). Growth Strategies. *Handbook of Economic Growth, 1,* 967–1014.

Roland, G. (2016, January). *Culture, Institutions and Development.* Namur January 2016 Conference.

Rostow, W. W. (1960). *The Stages of Growth: A Non-Communist Manifesto* (pp. 4–16). Cambridge: Cambridge University Press.

Sachs, J. D., & Warner, A. M. (2001). The Curse of Natural Resources. *European Economic Review, 45*(4–6), 827–838.

Schwartz, S. H. (1999). A Theory of Cultural Values and Some Implications for Work. *Applied Psychology, 48*(1), 23–47.

Serageldin, I., & Tabaroff, J. (1992). *Culture and Development in Africa. Proceedings of an International Conference Held at the World Bank.* Washington, DC: The World Bank.

Solow (1956). A Contribution to the Theory of Economic Growth. *Quarterly Journal of Economics, 70*(1), 65–94.

Tabellini, G. (2008, April–May). Institutions and Culture. Presidential Address by Guido Tabellini at the European Economics Association. *Journal of the European Economic Association, 6*(2–3), 255–294.

Tabellini, G. (2010). Culture and Institutions: Economic Development in the Regions of Europe. *Journal of the European Economic Association, 8*(4), 677–716.

Taras, V., Kirkman, B. L., & Steel, P. (2010). Examining the Impact of Culture's Consequences: A Three-Decade, Multilevel, Meta-Analytic Review of Hofstede's Cultural Value Dimensions. *Journal of Applied Psychology, 95*(3), 405–439.

Todaro, M. P., & Smith, S. C. (2006). *Economic Development* (8th ed.). Manila: Pearson South Asia Pte. Ltd.

Yew, L. K. (2000). *From Third World to First: The Singapore Story, 1965–2000: Singapore and the Asian Economic Boom.* New York: HarperCollins Publishers.

CHAPTER 4

Corruption and Culture in Ghana: Mission Impossible or an Interesting Challenge

Abstract This chapter focused on the inter-relationships between culture and corruption as it applies to Ghana. It used short stories/anecdotes to describe how a culture of apathy that has seeped into Ghanaian economic realities is creating opportunities for corruption and making the development challenge harder to confront. It discussed the literature suggestions about how to handle perverse culture that seems to nurture corruption and hamper growth. The chapter then identified the limitations of the literature suggestions and the plausible alternatives that offer more pragmatic avenues for limiting corruption by directly trying to undermine or change perverse cultural practices through changing mindsets via education, leadership with integrity and the smart use of technology.

Keywords Apathy • Mindsets • Education • Corruption and culture

Robert Lucas, the Nobel Prize–winning economist once remarked: "Once one starts to talk about growth, it is difficult to talk about anything else" (Lucas 1990). In contemporary Sub-Saharan Africa (SSA), however, it seems more pragmatic to say, "once one starts to talk about corruption, it is impossible to talk about anything else; certainly not growth." When told that President Nana Addo of Ghana was championing a "Ghana beyond Aid agenda", the Netherlands Ambassador to Ghana Ron Stryker remarked "Why not Ghana beyond Corruption" agenda (Strykker 2019). Other Ghanaians and Africans are tired of talking about corruption.

The reason is simple. Despite an endowment of significant mineral resources (gold, diamonds, bauxite, cobalt, iron, uranium and copper), oil, timber and cash crops (coffee, cocoa, cotton and tea) that should serve as the resource base for production and spur growth, SSA's growth performance from the post-independence years to the 1990s was unimpressive (Ndulu and O'Connell 2007; Bates 2006).

The economies of SSA post-independence, such as Ghana, were instead bogged down by corruption, which, in turn, catalyzed several violent uprisings, forceful military takeovers or coup d'états (Aryeetey and Kanbur 2016; Bates 2006).

Instead of serving as an input for sustained growth and development as has been the case for Norway, for example (see Armah 2016), SSA's resource endowment turned into what Sachs and Warner (2001) described as "the curse of natural resources" or "the resource curse" for short. SSA's resources seem to doom it to under-development. The reason for this some have claimed is corruption.

On one hand, the SSA situation seems to be improving with less conflicts per year reported in SSA over the last decade (Straus 2012; Burbach 2016). This follows decades of bloody conflict in the late 1980s, 1990s and 2000s over government corruption in dealing with revenues from natural resources such as diamond in countries like Liberia, Sierra Leone and the Congo.

Despite the decline in actual conflicts, news reports in 2019 by Cable News Network (CNN), British Broadcasting Corporation (BBC) among others indicate that the number of demonstrations in parts of Africa such as Sudan and Tunisia seems to on the increase, fueled by accusations of corruption, similar to the type of accusations that led to the Arab Spring.

Corruption is not unique to Africa (Nye 1967; Glynn et al. 1997). Far from it. Corruption defined broadly in this book as "the abuse of the public trust for private gain" has been the subject of intense research by economists at least for the last half century because of its reputation as a major obstacle to growth (Treisman 2000; Sandholtz and Taagepera 2005; World Bank 1993; Rose-Ackerman 1999; Sandholtz and Koetzle 2000; Sandholtz and Gray 2003; Waterbury 1973).

Corruption can arise in both private and government sectors as the word "public" in this book is not used to refer exclusively to government. "Public" in this book refers to a group of people governed by the same legal arrangement or consensus policies. For example, in the case of a private university, governed by university policies, if a professor takes a bribe from a student to inflate grades, the professor has abused the trust of "the public" which in this case is "the university community" for his personal gain. This is an act of corruption although it is in a private, not a government, institution.

In Africa the effects of corruption are exceptionally acute because the continent lacks public infrastructure and social amenities such as roads, bridges, overpasses, drains, stable electricity, clean water, health facilities, health personal, access to the internet and good jobs. This means corrupt acts by public officials that re-direct government funds to private pockets and prevent any of these infrastructure projects from completion affect the ability of the people to undertake economic activity in a severe way. For example, poor farmers cannot take their harvest to market if public officials, through corrupt acts, deplete the funds needed to build the road.

Although some of the stories of corruption in African countries are quite brazen, they are often linked to the political system in most of Africa where the economic life cannot be divorced from politics; departing governments are hardly ever held accountable to any serious degree for their wrongdoings. This happens probably because of fear of reprisals if they come back to power in a future election cycle.

As Daniel Jordan Smith carefully documented in her book about everyday corruption in Nigeria, stories of corruption in Nigeria, for example, are not only common and widespread but sometimes quite brazen (Smith 2007). To a large extent such acts of corruption are found in Ghana although the scale may be lower.

Smith (2007) recounts his own difficulties in dealing with corrupt government officials in state institutions as he tried to get a driver's license. His interactions with Nigerian civil servants revealed several acts of corruption among the police and government officials. These experiences are not uncommon in Ghana.

Nigeria and Ghana are not the only African countries saddled with corruption. South Africa, Kenya, Uganda, Liberia, Malawi, Gambia and most of English-speaking Africa, which is the focus of this book, have all had to deal with significant acts of corruption at the level of the state and at the level of the individual. This is not to imply that French-speaking Africa is any less corrupt. In fact, some scholars believe Francophone Africa may be significantly more corrupt than English-speaking West African countries.

Almost all the Sub-Saharan African countries except perhaps Botswana, Mauritius and Rwanda are regarded as among the most corrupt countries in the world. According to the 2018 ranking of Transparency International's Corruption Perception Index (CPI), which ranks countries with least corrupt countries first, Botswana, Rwanda and Mauritius ranked respectively 37th, 52nd and 59th out of 183 countries compared to Ghana's 82nd, Nigeria's 150th and Congo's 170th.

Not surprisingly, all three less corrupt SSA countries, Botswana, Rwanda and Mauritius, are strong long-run growth performers in a very corrupt neighborhood, at least by the standards of Transparency International's Corruption Perception Index (CPI). Botswana and Mauritius both have high real GDP per capita income levels. In fact, Botswana enjoyed more than 30 years of very fast growth post-independence in the 1960s to the 2000s exactly when the rest of Africa performed worst.

Focusing on Ghana for the sake of illustration, a little history is not out of place. Ghana is famous among the SSA countries for its remarkable stability, enduring freedoms and tolerant democracy which accommodates different tribes or ethnicities, religions and political dispensations in a very heterogeneous society (Armah 2016). However, even for Ghana, a country ranked higher than several Western countries in terms of peace stability and media freedom, corruption is a persistent and nagging issue.

Kwame Nkrumah led Ghana to independence as the first black African nation to do so and is a hallowed hero of Pan-Africanism. However, after serving as Ghana's first president on the ticket of the Convention People's Party (CPP), he was deposed in 1966 by a military coup led by top military officials because he was accused of unspeakable acts of corruption and abuse of office.

The accusations of corruption against Nkrumah included wasting away the nation's resources in grand projects and giving away millions of Ghana's wealth to other African nations who were then fighting for independence in an ambitious bid to unite, and then rule the whole of Africa. Nkrumah's ministers were also alleged to be notorious for their corruption with some of them (the famous Krobo Edusei, who was alleged not to have received formal education) rumored to sleep on a bed made of pure gold.

Nkrumah died in 1972, and there is not much evidence, since his death that has been unearthed about his own corruption but his reputation of authoritarian rule including declaring himself life president and his inability to reign in his ministers who were corrupt was most likely what precipitated his downfall.

The governments that followed Nkrumah such as those led by Brigadier Akwasi Afrifa, Dr. Kofi Abrefa Busia, Colonel Ignatius Kutu Acheampong and General Fred Akuffo were all ultimately deposed after accusations of either egregious acts of corruption or failure to act, where corruption existed, or when corruption occurred. Clearly, despite a seemingly benign attitude toward corruption, Ghanaians have taken drastic actions in the past to stop corruption but stopping corruption has proven elusive thus far in contemporary times.

Riding on a strong anti-corruption sentiment, fueled by popular socialist ideas at the time, Flt. Lt. J. J. Rawlings led a popular uprising in Ghana, as the head of the Armed Forces Revolutionary Council (AFRC) in 1979. The AFRC deposed incumbent Head of State at the time, General Fred Akuffo, who had himself deposed Colonel (now General Ignatius Kutu Acheampong) in 1978, less than a year before Rawlings and his men took power by force in 1979. Rawlings justified removing Akuffo by charging him with corruption just as Akuffo had charged Acheampong with corruption and removed him from office.

In fact, Rawlings and the AFRC went as far as to execute by firing squad, all living ex-military rulers of Ghana as well as the most senior officers in Fred Akuffo's government. According to a report by Myjoyonline:

> In 1979, General I.K. Acheampong, Major General E.K. Utuka, Rear Admiral Joy K. Amedume, Major General Kotei, General F.W.K. Akuffo, Air Vice Marshal George Yaw Boakye, Lt. Gen. Akwasi Amankwa Afrifa and Col. Roger J. Felli, were summarily executed by firing squad at the Teshie Shooting Range in Accra amidst chants of 'Let the blood flow' by some disgruntled Ghanaians. (Myjoyonline 2018)

Captain Boakye-Gyan, co-conspirator of Rawlings and co-chairman of the AFRC, explained decades later that those who were executed were killed for treason, or in simple language, for deposing legally elected governments in Ghana.

This meant that Colonel Ignatius Kutu Acheampong (later General Acheampong) who deposed elected President Dr. Kofi Abrefa Busia was guilty as was Brigadier (later General) Akwasi Amankwah Afrifa who together with Colonel (later Major General) Emmanuel Kotoka had deposed elected President Dr. Kwame Nkrumah.

Colonel Emanuel Kwasi Kotoka helped depose Nkrumah but was assassinated in 1967 in an abortive coup by junior officers of Ghana's Armed Forces stationed in Ho in the Volta region code named "Operation Guitar Boy" (Wiki 2019).

In comparison, Major General Joseph Arthur Ankrah who was the army commander at the time Nkrumah was removed from power and who ruled Ghana after Nkrumah departed from 1966 to 1969 was not killed because he was not a coup plotter. Lieutenant-Colonel Kotoka and Major Akwasi Amankwa Afrifa plotted and executed the 1966 coup that toppled Nkrumah but asked the Army general to rule as Head of State as he was the most senior military officer.

General Akwasi Afrifa who assumed power from 1969 to 1970 and oversaw the election that handed over power to President Kofi Abrefa Busia was alive but retired and was living in his village. Soldiers fetched Afrifa from his village in the Ashanti region to Accra, the capital. General Akwasi Afrifa was executed by the AFRC along with former military leaders General Acheampong and General Akuffo.

Other senior military officers including General Kotei, Rear Admiral Amedume, Air Vice Marshall Yaw Boakye, Colonel Feli and Captain Utuka were also executed for corruption with Ghanaian newspapers printing the now infamous and chilling words "let the blood flow" in support of the bloodletting (Myjoyonline, June 2018). Corruption is no laughing matter in Ghana as even the powerful elite, such as the country's leaders have actually paid the ultimate price for it.

President Hilla Liman, who assumed power after winning the elections supervised by Flt. Lt. Rawlings and his AFRC in 1979, was himself accused by Rawlings of corruption, and failure to act when corruption occurred. He was deposed in a military coup led by Rawlings in 1981.

Rawlings described the takeover in 1981 as a revolution (the 31 December Revolution): a cleansing of corruption from society and a rebirth of the nation with the army in the street enforcing strict laws including price control laws. Rawlings ruled Ghana from 1981 to 1992 and handed over power to himself as the presidential candidate of the National Democratic Congress (NDC) in an election in which the opposition New Patriotic Party (NPP) led by Professor Adu Boahen boycotted citing serious breaches of the law, vote rigging and corruption.

To his credit, Rawlings handed over power after two terms in office as president and head of the ruling National Democratic Congress (NDC) to President John Kufour, a former Rawlings appointee and a lawyer who, interestingly, fundamentally disagreed with and ruled very differently from Rawlings. John Kufour came to power on the ticket of the New Patriotic Party (NPP).

Ironically, Rawlings was himself accused of egregious acts of corruption while in office including selling state properties to his cronies and allowing his wife to take over state properties such as the Nsawam Cannery. Even though Rawlings has always denied wrongdoings and there is no smoking gun pointing to his crimes, the wealth accumulated by his ministers and appointees suggests there was some corruption going on. These former ministers are now rumored to be among the wealthiest men in Ghana and have been accused of abusing their power for economic gain. In some cases, they are rumored to have surprised Rawlings himself with the extent and impunity of their corruption.

President John Kufuor, who took over from Rawlings, is credited with tripling the country's real per capita income and discovering oil in commercial quantities for Ghana. However, Kufour was also accused of corrupt acts although never proven. For example, he was accused of selling valuable state lands to his family members at a pittance to develop hotels and other properties. A minister in Kufour's government was arrested and jailed in the USA on drug-related charges of corruption.

President John Mills succeeded John Kufuor in 2008 on the ticket of the NDC but died in office in 2012 as the only sitting president in Ghana who has ever died in office. John Mills was also vilified not because he himself was corrupt, but for appointing very young and corrupt politicians with no work experience to high offices. This happened presumably because Mills had a disagreement with Rawlings, who founded the NDC, so the older politicians in the NDC who were aligned with Rawlings did not want to work with Mills. The young politicians appointed by President Mills quickly amassed wealth under an aging and sick Mills who could not reign them in.

There is still little evidence that Mills himself was corrupt, but there are several accusations of the corrupt actions of his appointees. Some of the accusations include taking bribes before issuing contracts, over-pricing of projects and paying out government money for non-existent contracts claimed by their friends and cronies. A typical example is the now much-discussed Agbesi Woyome case.

Agbesi Woyome managed to convince government officials serving under Mills to pay him 51 million Ghana Cedis (equivalent of 51 million USD at the time) in judgment debt for breach of contract for a contract that never existed (Ghanaweb, August 2018).

The Ghanaian currency was at par with the dollar at the time so 51 million Ghana Cedis translated directly into 51 million USD. As Woyome was one of the biggest bankrollers of the ruling NDC at the time, the public outcry about corruption that followed was expected. The Woyome corruption scandal probably played a key role in framing the public perception of corruption in the NDC which resulted in a change of government in 2016 with the NDC's John Mahama losing out to the NPP's Nana Akuffo Addo.

President John Mahama was the serving Vice President under Mills when the latter died. Mahama took over as president, upon the demise of Mills and ruled from 2012 to 2016 after winning the 2012 elections. John Mahama was also accused of presiding over the most corrupt presidency in Ghana's history though this was never officially proven. It is alleged that he famously signed off 70% of the country's entire endowment of bauxite worth a colossal $180 billion to a company owned by his brother, Ibrahim Mahama. Both brothers claimed that the deal was above board, but the conflict of interest is self-evident (Ghanaweb 2019).

Mahama did not help his cause by presiding over a presidency where there were several accusations of state monies invested in projects literally evaporating. In one example, it was alleged that money invested in raising guinea fowls in Northern Ghana could not be retrieved because the guinea fowls flew to Burkina Faso. President Mahama is also accused of a failure to deal with the two most serious challenges that Ghana had faced in its history until the time: Illegal gold mining by illegal Chinese miners ("Chinese Galamsey") and the Power Crisis "or Dum Sor" where Ghanaians did not have access to stable electricity for a year (2013–2014).

Both challenges were alleged to be linked to corruption. In the case of illegal mining, there were suggestions that some of the Ministers under Mahama benefitted from the largesse of some of the Chinese criminals and rather threatened Ghanaian citizens who dared ask questions (Daily Guide). The electric power crisis was alleged to be essentially linked to debt overhang due to non-payment by government institutions and corrupt acts that depleted government funds intended to pay for electric power.

President John Mahama was followed by current President Nana Akuffo Addo who enjoys a reputation as an incorruptible president. However, President Akuffo Addo is currently under fire, not for his own corruption, because there is no evidence of that, but for the alleged (even if not proven) corruption of his appointees such as the former director of the Ghana Revenue Service (GRA), the Minister of Sports and one of the Deputy Ministers of Sports in 2019.

While the former head of the GRA was accused of rehabilitating a government bungalow for his own use to the tune of several thousands of dollars including purchasing 11 air-conditioners for a two-bedroom flat during his term as the head of another government institution (see the Herald 2018), questions were raised about the expenditure report of the national soccer team, the Black Stars, in the 2019 African Cup of Nations submitted by the Minister of Sports to Parliament.

For his part, in several radio reports, the Deputy Minister of Sports was accused of being complicit in a bizarre incident where some Ghanaian were deported from Australia after posing as journalists to cover the Commonwealth Games in 2018.

Despite his visionary leadership, strong character and obvious humanity, Akuffo Addo's reactions to accusations of corruption by his appointees have raised questions since in each case, the government has exonerated the accused wrongdoer and absolved the person of all wrongdoing by simply issuing a white paper following an internal investigation absolving them of blame. In effect, no one has been punished. The perception of the public is that all these people cannot be innocent especially since some information about these corrupt acts was already out in the public domain.

In a very ironic twist, former President John Mahama, having secured the nomination as the presidential candidate for the National Democratic Congress (NDC), the biggest opposition party for the fast-approaching 2020 elections, is currently leading a crusade accusing incumbent President Akuffo Addo of corruption. Mahama is hoping to regain power by accusing Akuffo Addo of corruption, or inaction where corruption occurs: the very thing that Akuffo Addo accused him off and which helped the latter win the presidency from him.

Clearly corruption is a headache to African countries and Ghana is no exception. Some scholars have suggested that the root of the problem may be found in some of Africa's cultural values and beliefs. Of course this is a controversial statement and highly offensive to some anthropologists and Africanists. However, to identify effective developmental strategies for Africa, a hands-off approach to culture is doomed to fail. It is worth investigating the inter-relationships between some of these cultural values, beliefs and practices on one hand, and corruption and development on the other hand.

For example, while several traditional practices such as gift giving especially to leaders and royalty are an expected symbol of reverence, they may easily be misconstrued for corruption in the Western sense. At worst, such practices could be nurturing corruption as they set unrealistic expectations.

It is rumored that President John Mahama of Ghana allegedly gave a particularly illustrative example of the danger of misinterpreting cultural practices as corruption from a Western point of view. When he was accused of accepting a large Sports Utility Vehicle (a Cadillac Escalade valued at $100,000) from a contractor he had awarded a contract to (see Manasseh 2016), he replied that he had to accept several gifts from the chiefs of different tribes he visits in Ghana in his official capacity as President of Ghana. He has to accept cows, goats and so forth, otherwise he will offend the giver. If he does not accept them, it will be traditionally the highest form of insult to these chiefs and their people. The implied question he was imposing was simply: what is the difference between a cow and car? They are both gifts and can influence people. His point about the role of culture in explaining acts that can be perceived to be corrupt I think is clear.

Further, the different and very many tribes in African countries often generate corruption-related behavior where the perpetrators justify their action as seeking the interest of their particular tribesmen or seeking to put their clansmen in positions of power to benefit the clan or tribe instead of the nation. Government appointments are often tribalistic instead of meritocratic undermining efficiency.

According to Schleifer and Vishny (1993) and proponents of the principal agent theory of corruption (Becker and Stigler 1974, Rose-Ackerman 1975, 1978, 1999; Krueger 1974; Banfield 1985; Klitgaard 1988, 1991), the government officials or the agents of developing countries such as those in SSA do not act in the interest of the principal, or the public, for whom they are supposed to be serving. Rather, they serve their own selfish interest while the public is impoverished. These interests may sometimes be those of their tribe and not personal interest, but it is still not aligned with the national interest, so it is considered corruption. In some SSA countries, corruption is probably a significant portion of GDP (Schleifer and Vishny 1993).

Africa's long struggle for development, and battle against corruption even after taking on board Western ideas of democratization, absorbing foreign aid and implementing policies of economists from Breton-woods institutions like the World Bank and International Monetary Fund (IMF) seem to suggest there is something else missing in making the advice of such experts more effective in Africa.

One possible factor may be culture. This is not surprising as the economics literature itself, until recently, ignored culture as a significant determinant of corruption or development in general because of definitional and measurement issues and a lack of data (Guiso et al. 2015; Alesina and Giuliano 2015). This means the advice of development economists based on formal theory inherently did not consider the cultural context.

However, for the reason that culture seems so important to the African and to the Ghanaian in particular (the Akans say "yen sei amamere" or "we don't destroy culture" and the Gas say "kusuum gboo" to wit "culture and tradition never dies"), it makes sense to analyze the possible contribution of culture in explaining corruption and development in Ghana.

This chapter focuses on the possible interactions between culture and corruption that are relevant for developmental objectives and have been the subject of vigorous research, more recently, after the "hands off" attitude of economic theory in the past toward the economics of culture. Emphasis is placed on Ghana.

Before we proceed, it may make sense to define culture again. Defining culture, however, is an arduous task made even more difficult by overlapping the definition of culture and institutions (Alesina and Giuliano 2015). Dutch Psychologist Geert Hofstede defines culture as "the programming of the mind that separates one group of people from another" (Hofstede 1980, 1990, 2001; Hofstede et al. 2010).

Defining corruption is also very difficult (Mauro 1995). For the purposes of this chapter, we follow Rose-Ackerman (1978) and others and define corruption as "the abuse of the public trust for private gain" (Mauro 1995; Schleifer and Vishny 1993; Rose-Ackerman 1978; Kaufmann and Wei 1999).

Different definitions of corruption exist. Corruption can have different intensities, take many forms and manifest in both the private and public. We will avoid semantics and stick to the working definition we have already provided: "corruption is the abuse of the public trust for private gain." While corruption can become endemic and develop into a persistent culture of corruption, it still pays to investigate the factors that generate corruption, aggravate it or nurture it in order to be able to explain how corruption undermines development.

I concede that corruption is an age-old problem with a long history (Leff 1964, Krueger 1974; Rose-Ackerman 1978, 1999, 2004; Banerjee 1999; Bardhan 1997; Treisman 2000; Mauro 1995; Fisman and Miguel 2007; Schleifer and Vishny 1993; Olken 2007; Kaufmann 1997). Corruption can be traced back several millennia. As Bardhan (1997) reports in his review of the corruption literature, Kautilya, a public administrator in ancient India is documented to have recorded in his Arthashastra "just as it is impossible not to taste the honey (or the poison) that finds itself at the tip of the tongue. So it is impossible for a government servant not to eat up, at least, a bit of the King's revenue" (Kautilya, 4 BC as quoted in Bardhan 1997).

According to former United Nations (UN) secretary general, Kofi Annan, "corruption is an insidious plague that has a wide variety of corrosive effects on societies. It undermines democracy and the rule of law; leads to violations of human rights; distorts markets; erodes quality of life, and allows organized crime, terrorism and other threats to human security to flourish" (Annan 2004). Gould (1991) is even more emphatic: "Corruption is an immoral and unethical phenomenon that contains a set of moral aberrations from moral standards of society, causing loss of respect for and confidence in duly constituted authority."

Clearly corruption is serious business in Africa and a key issue in the Ghanaian context. Corruption must be understood fully and in the cultural context in order to be able to minimize some of its harmful effects. This chapter uses short story sketches to illustrate how culture and corruption interact to determine development outcomes in Ghana because of the reverence Ghanaians attach to their culture. It is possible that previous neoliberal Bretton-Woods type policy advice to Ghana has failed because it ignored Ghanaian culture. A fundamental mistake.

From what this author knows of Ghanaians, they would most likely ignore the advice of an expert who does not take Ghanaian cultural values into account. This means Western economic advice and policies, even if they were credible, were dead on arrival in Ghana if they simply ignored Ghanaian culture.

Ignoring Ghanaian culture in giving policy advice to Ghanaian policymakers is not as far-fetched as it first sounds. As discussed earlier, a long tradition of economists make "the ceteris paribus" assumptions and ignore culture although it may be variations in culture that provides the answers to making the policy advice more effective. Given that the economic literature itself is now re-focusing on culture, it makes sense to reconsider culture in talking about corruption in Ghana.

The chapter is motivated by the conclusions of Huntington (2000) who compared the real GDP per capita of Ghana and South Korea in the 1960s, when these two countries first became independent. He compared South Korea and Ghana again when he visited both countries in the 1990s and compared their contemporary performances to that in the late 1990s when he first visited both countries. He found that the real GDP per capita of South Korea was 15 times larger than that of Ghana.

To explain the more than 15-times difference in the real GDP per capita of these two countries, Huntington (2000) appealed to cultural differences. He explained that since these two countries were very similar at independence (in terms of total population, population growth rate, literacy rates, amounts of foreign aid received etc.), South Korea's relatively stronger performance was most likely due to South Korea's more effective cultural values (Huntington 2000; Heffner 2002).

Huntington (2000) wrote that the difference in performance over time was expected because "while the South Koreans valued saving, discipline, organization, investment, hard work, thrift and education, Ghanaians had other values."

It is difficult to surmise why Huntington (2000) settled on "perverse culture" as the most important factor to explain the income difference instead of the more popular reason of "weak institutions" that was so popular around the time that he was writing, championed by Acemoglu, Johnson and Robinson (2001) among others.

I can only guess that it was because Huntington (2000) himself had conducted research where he seemed to emphasize the role of culture. It could also be that he had familiarized himself with both Ghanaian culture and South Korean culture and he was more comfortable talking about the cultural difference.

Alesina and Giuliano (2015) have illustrated the similarity between the definitions of culture and institutions. According to them, culture is actually "informal institutions" while institutions are "formal institutions" so separating the two concepts has been difficult historically. So, although Huntington (2000) ascribed the differential performance between Ghana and South Korea after one generation to culture, he may well have implied institutions as well.

In any case, Huntington (2000) is entitled to his opinion. He probably visited Ghana on both occasions when the country had a functioning democracy. He ignored the influence of the many military coup d'états that Ghana has suffered and what if any, the effects of the interchanging periods of military rule and civilian democratic rule had on not just Ghana's institutions and culture but on the incentives for corruption and development. So, while culture may have had something to do with Ghana's below par performance, and aggravated corruption, the story is likely a much more complicated one.

Ghana's weaker performance compared to South Korea cannot be explained by simply assuming that Ghanaians are a bunch of "undisciplined, disorganized spendthrifts who do not save, are indolent, do not invest and do not value education" without trying to understand why that may be so even if that is so.

If the implied assertion that Ghanaians were "undisciplined, disorganized, spendthrifts, who do not save, are indolent, do not invest and do not value education" was true, it will explain, at least in part, the differential performance. The problem is that the veracity of Huntington's (2000) statement is hard to establish because it will be practicaly difficult and politically offensive to do so. Further, even if true, it cannot explain away all the differences between the performance of Ghana and South Korea.

Of the negative traits that Huntington (2000) ascribed to Ghana, the most difficult one to justify is education. Ghana is littered with stories of people who gained education only because their families sold all they had to finance it. In some instances, a whole village has sold its lands and properties to send a few bright members of the family abroad for the purposes of education. Ghanaians love education. Ghana exported so many teachers and nurses to other parts of Africa in the past including to Nigeria and Uganda. Kwame Nkrumah, the first president of Ghana, hid in a ship to go to the USA so that he could get an education. Ghanaians have always loved and still love education.

I think the type of education that Ghanaians have reached for has been white collar, desk-sitting service jobs and that is probably worth discussing. This is probably a reflection of the less effective math education in the country compared to South Korea. The choice of the kind of education to focus on, and how effective the education is, is important in determining developmental outcomes. A country that focuses on math education has a higher chance of being involved in technology-intensive (Science, Technology Engineering and Math or STEM) research compared to one where math is avoided. The former country will clearly be more productive as it will learn how to use and how to develop new productivity-enhancing technology.

One other factor Huntington (2000) overlooked in explaining the difference in performance between South Korea and Ghana is the extent of American influence in South Korea and the limited American influence in Ghana given Ghana often leaned socialist. Apart from offering different opportunities for South Koreans to study in the USA, in the Cold War era, the USA also provided South Korea with substantial amount of aid, compared to Ghana, in terms of both technical assistance and finance in the 30 years subsequent to Huntington's (2000) visit in the post-independence period. This makes sense because of the Cold War dynamics as the USA was in competition with the Union of Soviet Socialist Republic (USSR) to win minds and both North and South Korea were relevant battlegrounds. There was a need for the USA to keep South Korea, which was under US influence, competitive, compared to North Korea under USSR in this battle of ideologies.

South Korea, to their credit, invested in education and ensured that each citizen obtained quality education to post-secondary level. That may account for their superior achievement in terms of productivity and development, compared to Ghana.

However, it is also true that South Koreans are a homogenous people. They are all Koreans and speak a common language and have a common culture: Korean culture. Even though Korea as a country had a civil war and was split in two, South Korea as an independent country comprised of the same ethnic group with similar political ideology. In contrast, Ghana is a hotbed of different tribes with different agenda and a history of inter-tribal conflict. Ghana has upward of 100 tribes (Wiki) speaking different languages but living relatively closely to each either in the same institutional framework and governance structure.

Such a situation, as found in Ghana, has the potential to incentivize tribal politics, where loyalties are declared with associated sycophancy undermining the effectiveness of institutions and thwarting developmental efforts because it sets the different groups against each other. Ghana, or indeed Africa, is not the only place where tribalism has undermined development. It has been responsible for wars in Kosovo and Eastern Europe as well. More recently, Myanmar has been accused of trying to wipe out the ethnic Rohingya Moslems. Tribalism can be dangerous. To underestimate its corrosive effect is to miss a key determinant of corruption.

It may interest Huntington (2000) to also observe that Ghanaians are extremely friendly, and super tolerant of different tribes, identities, races and religions. Ghanaians are also extremely empathetic. It is also true that Ghanaians for millennia have been champions of keeping the peace. Ghana has been consistently ranked among the top five most peaceful countries in Africa for the last several decades. Ghana has never had a war in the post-independence period which is impressive for a SSA country. A conversation with elderly Ghanaians would have quickly revealed to Huntington that a deeply entrenched belief of the Ghanaian is that "the wise keep the peace through a combination of tolerance and forgiveness."

Unfortunately, it may be also true, though, that it is this empathy and willingness to concede and forgive "to keep the peace" that Ghanaians are famed for, and are so proud of, that are nurturing cultural traits "different" from what Huntington noticed in South Korea and could be nurturing corruption.

Keeping the peace can sometimes imply simply "kicking the can further down the road." Even in a trusting society, if individuals learn they will be forgiven, literally 77 times as the Christian Bible says, lessons are hard to learn. Offenders may re-commit the same crimes because the threat of punishment is either non-existent or not credible. Those entrusted by the public to manage the nation's wealth may abuse that trust knowing they will be forgiven even if exposed. Such a cultural disposition will inadvertently nurture corruption.

Another factor that Huntington (2000) ignored was that Ghana had been influenced by several different ideologies and cultures in the 30 years following independence, which was his frame of reference. Ghana had been subjected to Kwame Nkrumah's Scientific Socialism, then to long periods of military rule before the current democratic dispensation that started in 1992. Ultimately, such experiences tend to influence what Hofstede (1980) describes as "the programming of the mind" or Ghanaian culture. Even if culture changes slowly, it does change so Huntington should have considered such dynamism in his analysis.

Despite some of the criticisms against Huntington's (2000) conclusion, it may be difficult to disagree with some of the essential argument he is making. It could well be true that South Korea is much more productive than Ghana because of historical and contemporary influences as well as more effective leadership that has enabled them to nurture a culture that focuses on *"hard work, thrift, discipline, organization, savings and education,"* while Ghana, in comparison, may have had different influences, and probably did not benefit as effectively from a succession of leaders.

Ghana also suffered intermittent military and civilian rule at a time where South Koreans were uniting behind their leaders in a Cold War common belief that South Korea's democratic outcome must trump communist North Korean performance. Ghana's experience with intermittent military and civilian rule has consequences for corruption and growth.

According to Murdoch (2009), the transition from autocratic to democratic rule can significantly distort the culture of a people, and worsen corruption, as significant restraints and controls imposed by the state are relaxed in the transition process from military to civilian rule. This is as true for the change to democratic rule from communist rule as it is for the change from military dictatorship to democracy.

In the case of the change from military rule to civilian rule, where the incumbent military leader hands power over to himself as a democratic leader, the problems with institutions are often more acute. This is because the military leader who is handing power over to himself as a civilian ruler will have strong incentives to ensure that the new constitution that will guide his rule as a civilian president will enable him to retain most of his absolute powers. This likely happened in Ghana and may explain what Armah (2016) identified as Ghana's weak institutions.

Unfortunately, the period of change from autocratic, military rule to democratic civilian rule is often associated with a significant increase in corruption as key players take advantage of less strict control by the state to abuse public trust for private gain. In fact, the citizens may develop apathy toward issues relating to nationalism as they find themselves free of the autocratic demands for loyalty to the nation. There is likely to be more abuse of the public trust and less monitoring of deviant behavior which previously will be harshly and swiftly punished by the autocratic regime.

This can lead to a dangerous feeling of apathy that will then stimulate not only corruption but also some of the behavior traits Huntington described: *indiscipline, disorganization, and indolence and ultimately corruption.*

Ghanaians in this frame of mind may well say "enye hwee" to wit "it does not matter" in response to unhelpful practices they notice others do because they have become apathetic. Given that Ghana is also known for its empathy, a dangerous mixture of apathy toward productive ventures and corruption and empathy to forgive corrupt behavior seems reflective of, at least on the surface, Huntington's (2000) charge of "indiscipline and disorganization" and will lead to corruption.

Such a culture of "apathy" and "excessive empathy" will most likely hold Ghana back for generations and ultimately prove Huntington (2000) correct if such a culture does not evolve, guided by education, technology and effective leadership with integrity into something with less perverse consequences.

TIME FOR SOME SHORT STORIES IN TRUE GHANAIAN TRADITION

Let's now re-acquaint ourselves with the characters from the first part of this book. Two friends from college (an American and a Ghanaian) re-unite in Ghana, 25 years after graduating from an American college where they were roommates and intimate friends. Such a reunion is a potentially stimulating and rewarding encounter.

Kofi, the Ghanaian, seized the opportunity to introduce Allen to Ghana and explained how aspects of the culture that helps in keeping the peace may be leading to apathy and aggravating corruption. Kofi does this through recounting some of his own experiences with the central theme running through them being the apathy that has engulfed the country in the post-military regime period and nurturing corruption.

Kofi explains through his narratives that the famous peace-loving and forgiving characteristic of Ghanaian culture is combining with the apathy evident from the post-military period of freedom to nurture indiscipline and give a sense of disorganization. This may not only directly push down productivity as it demotivates the people to work hard but create fertile grounds for corruption.

Ghana has had a functioning democracy since 1992 when military ruler and benign dictator Jerry John Rawlings handed over power to himself as an elected president. The freedom coming with that after initial state control where the state was the provider coupled with the very empathetic character of Ghanaians has led to a phenomenon this author terms "enye hwee" to mean "it does not matter" raising the incentives for corrupt behavior.

Kofi encourages Allen to respond with "enye hwee" if he detected apathy in a situation in each of the short stories he narrates in like manner to the naming of a child in Ghana. During the naming ceremony among the Ga, the indigenes of Ghana's capital, Accra, the Wulomo or fetish priest pours libation, utters some chants to which the crowd responds "yao!" to signal agreement almost like an "Amen."

The first story Kofi tells is of an itinerant, commercial peddler of local drugs, herbs and concoctions who travels in commercial vehicles selling formal prescription drugs in Ghana which is against the formal laws of Ghana.

The practice goes unchecked partly because of a very permissive and empathetic Ghanaian disposition toward the informal sector and an ineffective Ghana Standards Board (GSB) which hesitates whenever it deals with Ghana's large informal sector. There are unconfirmed stories of standard board officials accepting bribes instead of punishing such behavior. While there is no evidence that this is true, it does beg the question, "why has this practice persisted for so long?" For emphasis, we dramatize the exchange between Kofi and Allen.

Kofi: There is an interesting character who travels on these commercial buses selling medicines and anything from aspirin to Viagra. He gains the trust of the passengers by saying Christian prayers for the journey. In Ghana, which is one of most religious country in the world, such a service is widely appreciated. He then proceeds to sell his medicines for about ten minutes before asking the driver to let him off the bus.

The passengers enthusiastically buy from him. He offers several guarantees for some of his Western and foreign-made medicines. I therefore asked an older gentleman his opinion of such an act. I explained that this guy can inadvertently kill people who buy medicine from him without knowing the right dosage, application or side-effects.

This guy knows that he is not qualified to sell these drugs, but he is doing so just to make money. Most of the people, to whom he is selling, do not seem to be very well educated. The Ghana Standard Boards (GSB) has the mandate to stop and should stop this dangerous practice but they do not. Why?

Kofi: The old man looked at me as if to suggest that I should be more understanding as Ghana was a developing country. I should be more empathetic. Things are generally hard for everyone, so this peddler is also just trying to survive.

Old man: "Enye hwee" which translates "it does not matter" since the peddler has been selling drugs on commercial buses for long time now. In any case it was not my place to say.

Kofi: So, in brief Allen, when unqualified people sell medicines to Ghanaians for their own benefit and the Ghana Standard Board, entrusted by the public ignores this...

Allen: Enye hwee

Kofi: You are catching on fast. There is a sense of indiscipline and disorganization. Industries such as the drug industry seem a little disorganized because the sector is a melting pot that has so many moving parts. There is the formal health sector that uses trained medical doctors to make diagnosis and write prescriptions. This formal health sector uses trained pharmacists to serve prescriptions and trained nurses to take care of the sick. This is as good as it gets. This formal health sector has dynamic public and private sectors.

There is also the traditional health sector that uses herbs to cure the sick in the informal sector. Within this sector, there are traditional healers who heal through a mixture of herbs and voodoo. There are also spiritualists or Christians who offer healing through prayers. For example, they run camps where they chain mentally challenged people in the bush on the pretext of healing them through prayer, for an amount of money as fee. There are the evangelist priest who claim to heal through miracles and sell "holy water" and other concoctions which supposedly bring healing and riches. These priests are often on TV and purchase airtime to offer proof of their miracles by healing the sick and sometimes raising the dead.

There are also the itinerant medicine peddlers who roam from house to house and board public transportation in order to sell their medicines to passengers. Ghanaians can see these medicine peddlers in action, but I want you to guess what Ghanaians say when they notice this.

Allen:	"Enye hwee."
Kofi:	Exactly.
Allen:	So, are there any more interesting phenomenon in the health sector or this is as good as it gets?
Kofi:	Hold your horses. You are "drinking the soup from the ladder instead of the pot" as we say in Ghana. There is more. I visited the hospital just yesterday to ask for prescription malaria drugs that can prevent malaria. I waited outside the Outpatients Department (OPD) and engaged an old woman in conversation who happened to be a retired nurse.

She was complaining about how lax the system had become since the time of the revolution, where people were disciplined. Essentially this was because they were afraid of the military rulers, although less drugs were available then. Now people just say "enye hwee" and move on.

Old Woman:	Now the situation of discipline in the public hospital sector is terrible after we obtained democracy. I do not want to spoil any body's job by going to the media. They will call me an old witch and isolate me, but I see a lot of things. Nurses, mostly female, do not arrive to work on time and fear no punishment as they have befriended the doctors who are mostly male. Nurses and doctors who work in government hospitals routinely take medicines, syringes and other supplies home while doctors refer patients to their own private clinics or the clinics of other friends. I remember complaining to a patient and to my surprise guess how she responded.

Kofi: "Enye hwee."
Exactly. She could not be bothered, or she felt too powerless to act. On hearing the old woman's narration, Kofi asked if the private hospitals give better care.
Kofi: Do the private hospitals do a better job by giving care?
Retired Nurse: They charge a lot more so probably yes, but they all have a patient ward system that is confusing. Most of them rent out residential buildings and convert them to hospitals and clinics. The rooms in the hospital that act as hospital wards are often difficult to navigate and monitor.

However, to cut costs, they maintain a skeletal staff at the front who typically are on their phones all the time. They may go and check on patients in the night once or two times but there is no way to monitor if they do.

The hospitals could choose to buy Closed Circuit Cameras (CCT) to observe patients especially during the night shifts but choose not to do so citing cost. This often leads to death of patients. I remember asking a doctor in the local language about the need for CCT cameras in these private hospitals.

To my surprise, he answered that patients have bells they could ring if they needed help although a worker I knew at the hospital informed me that none of the bells worked. In any case I wondered how a sick person in trouble can correctly remember to ring a bell. I complained to a patient admitted to a hospital and to my surprise guess how she responded.

Kofi: "Enye hwee." Just leave it to God.
Kofi: That seems too improbable to be true. How can that stand. Is there not a medical board and a functioning government? Who checks this? People will be outraged by such a story. The hospital will be sued and maybe closed.
Retired Nurse: My son, this is Ghana, one of the most empathetic and most religious places on earth. People hardly ever get punished for their wrongdoing if they express remorse. Even if they do not express remorse, others will advocate on their behalf, beg for them, and they will be forgiven.

Not long ago, the medical board closed the hospital of a doctor who was not trained as a doctor but was practicing medicine. A few weeks later he re-opened his shop. I am not sure what happened but apparently it was the police that facilitated it. Some neighbors I talked to were resigned to it. Guess what they said?

Kofi: "Enye hwee."
Retired Nurse: My son, you forget there is a power imbalance between the patients and the doctors in terms of knowledge and economic status. Further, lawsuits are historically not common here; it is still not the culture. Even if it was, the private hospitals will have better representation than the patients.

Most important of all, people are very religious and see death as something more divine than physical. It is assumed the doctor would have done his best. There is less questioning about a doctor's action than you might think here. Sad, but true.

Unfortunately, some unscrupulous doctors are taking advantage of the disposition of the people. There are several media reports of doctors practicing without licenses. Does that not surprise you?

Do you know Anas, the famous Ghanaian investigative journalist who has revealed so much corruption in Ghana's health sector including illegal abortions being performed? He also did an exposé in the judiciary system, the police, the mining sector and the sports sector. I guess most Ghanaians are outraged by the seriousness of the corrupt acts but guess what others will say.

Kofi: "Enye hwee."
Kofi: It does surprise me and so does a lot of things about Ghana. I have not been around for many years, so I am still learning.
Old woman: Most people, especially in the informal sector, will respond "enye hwee." Let's not bother about it. That is the problem. There is a lot of apathy in the system. There is a lot of indiscipline and disorganization.

When Kofi finished narrating his story to his college roommate, Allen, he could sense that Allen was intrigued and wanted to experience more of the Ghanaian culture. Kofi decided to take Allen on a one-week trip that will include attending a funeral, going to a church and visiting his former primary school. They would also visit some private and public universities so that Allen can appreciate the burst in growth in the private university sector. The Ghanaian university sector was a public monopoly till 1993.

Kofi hired a taxi to take them on the trip. When their trip started Kofi noticed that Allen was reading Daniel Jordan Smith's book on everyday corruption in Nigeria, so he asked him about it.

Kofi: I have also read that book. It seems interesting. How far have you gone with it?

Allen: I am almost finished. I must say it must have been interesting to observe how public officers interact with Ghanaians and to watch the police interact with drivers as well.

Kofi: I will just tell you my opinion, but it is probably shared by a lot of Ghanaians. The story you just read in Daniel Jordan Smith's book is a good guide. I will say corruption has declined in Ghana somewhat as average incomes have edged up in the democratic period from 1992 to now. However, the indiscipline has gone up after military rule. Further, the last decade or more has seen the government turn to digital technology to reduce the discretionary powers of government officers in order to curb corruption. Digitalization has been introduced at the seaports (Ghana Ports and Harbors Authority or GHAPOHA), at the Driver and Licensing Authority (DVLA) and at the Passport office. This means the level of corruption is less than what you read in Daniel Jordan Smith's book.

However, there is still the perception among the public that these officers sometimes create undue delays just to frustrate people into paying bribes. There remain serious problems in offices such as Ghana Water, the public utility for water; the Lands Commission where land titles are registered and the divisions of the Metropolitan Authority, where building permits are issued. The perception of corruption in these offices is significantly higher among Ghanaians. The probability of obtaining a building permit in less than three years when one applies for a permit is almost zero.

Allen:	I see. The situation about the building permits is very similar to what I am reading in Daniel Jordan Smiths book. By the way, I see a police check point ahead. Are you sure all the car papers are up to date and the driver has a working license?
Driver:	Everything is alright except that my quarterly income tax is expired.
Allen:	How come? Surely you must pay taxes?
Driver:	Taxi drivers pay direct income taxes but most Ghanaians in the informal sector like masons, carpenters, hawkers, blacksmiths, welders, truck pushers, Kenkey and prepared food sellers do not pay direct income taxes. Taxi drivers pay several different amounts to different government agencies. We pay money for roadworthy fee to DVLA, vehicle insurance fee to insurance companies, association fees for the Taxi's parent Taxi rank, as well as the quarterly income tax to the Ghana Revenue Authority (GRA) through the metropolitan authority. I have paid for two quarters which ended on June 30th. Today is July 1st. I just did not have time to purchase the tax stamp and this is something you can only get by going to one of the offices. The lines are often long, and officers frustrate us to create bribery opportunities. We present daily accounts to our taxi owners, so this waste of time is big problem. Wait! here comes the police.
Police Office:	Good Afternoon. Where are you going? Please open your boot.
Kofi:	Allen, in Ghana boot means trunk.
Driver:	Ok here you are sir.
Police:	It's hot. Where are you guys going?
Driver:	To a funeral.
Police:	Sorry to hear that. However, your income tax ticket is expired.
Driver:	Yes, today is the first day of quarter 3. I did not have time to purchase it.
Police:	You are going to a funeral. There is always food, drink and entertainment there. Your brother is in the sun. You should make sure I am also comfortable.

Driver:	On our way back, we will take care of you. Right now, we are going to the funeral and we do not know what we will meet.
Police:	I will be off duty. Let us not drag this one. You must go to the funeral.
Driver:	Ok brother here you go. Yes, we must be on our way.

The taxi continued on its way. Allen, who had just read about the difficult interactions between police and drivers in Daniel Jordan Smith's book queried Kofi and the Driver:

Allen:	I know that money was exchanged there. However, will you call that extortion for money? The exchange was very civil.
Kofi:	I agree. There remains significant police corruption. In the urban areas there is a lot of spotlight by the media on police activities. Ghanaians also often post corrupt police behavior on social media sites, so corruption appears to be going down. In the rural areas, corruption by the police is worse but it is also less frequent. Ghana has very limited police presence in the rural areas. The rural area police as you saw are also not aggressive. It is almost a negotiation.
Allen:	I see.
Kofi:	We just arrived at the funeral grounds. Notice how all the women are dressed in a similar traditional style of "Kaba and Slit" and wearing the same dark-colored material? The men drape the same cloth around their bodies in the traditional style. In Ghana when someone dies, the family specifies the type of cloth to be worn and every sympathizer must buy the cloth, and have it sewn. Since the ceremony lasts more than a day, the cloth for particular days are different. Kofi proceeds to describe funerals in Ghana to Allen.
Kofi:	Attending a funeral is Ghana is a deeply cultural experience. Various tribes in Ghana have slight differences in their culture funeral but there is some uniformity in the rituals performed across tribes. The major difference in the conduct of funerals depends on the religion of the

deceased. While Ghanaian Moslems bury their dead the same day, Ghanaian Christian funerals are usually a mixture of religious and traditional ceremonies, are expensive and can last a long time. Focusing on the Christian funeral, which is more reflective of tradition, the original traditional arrangement was supposed to cut costs by involving the whole extended family in financing the funeral.

Rather, what the Ghanaian Christian funeral culture has involved into is an expensive ceremony where the children and family are expected to spare no expense to demonstrate how dear they hold the recently departed family member. There is great disgrace associated with not being able to deliver a plush funeral. The funeral itself is usually a three-day affair involving a wake-keeping on Friday night, burial on Saturday and Thanksgiving Service on Sunday. However, the body is usually kept refrigerated anywhere from two weeks to a few years depending on the wealth and status of the departed and the prominence of the family. The long period of time between death and burial allows the family to inform everyone and to drum up expectations for the funeral.

In Ghana, the cost of the funeral can often impoverish children of the deceased because the extended family often defers to the children of the deceased to pay all costs. Some family elders have been accused of corruption where they pocket funeral donations intended to defray funeral costs.

Kofi and Allen attended all the funeral ceremonies including the church service where Allen experienced for himself the vibrancy, singing and dancing in a Ghanaian church. Of course, Allen was a little surprised by the many times the pastor asked for the whole church body to give donations. Kofi explained that some of these donations will go to the family of the deceased but probably not all the donations will find their way to the correct pockets. The churches differed in terms of their appetite for harvesting liquidity from the congregation.

Following the funeral, Kofi originally planned to take Allen to visit his former primary school. There were some reports in the news about the declining quality of public education. Teachers were rumored to be unmotivated and will even take their children to private schools although they were teaching in public primary schools. This was surprising to Kofi as the primary school system when he was young was decent but again it was during military rule.

There were also unconfirmed stories of teachers not showing up for classes especially in the rural areas. Those who showed up will often be found doing calculations from recordings of previous scores of national lottery or "Lotto" numbers during class time. This apathy was probably a reflection of low salaries of these teachers but does not justify it. Rather misplaced empathy on the path of parents in these rural areas who themselves are often illiterate may account for this. Either way, such behavior by the teachers is an abuse of the public trust for their private gain and only survives in a cultural setting tolerant of such behavior.

Kofi explained to Allen that the corruption in the education sector was not limited to the primary school system. Apathy can also seep into the university system where a booming although relatively young private university sector was also struggling with its own unique corruption problems. Kofi therefore took Allen to visit Kwadwo, a friend from school and now a lecturer at a private university.

The conversation between Kofi and Kwadwo, a lecturer at the private university where Kofi had taken Allen for a visit, is quite illuminating.

Kofi:	Kwadwo, now that the private university sector is up and booming, lecturers must be enjoying job security. All university lecturers in Ghana do not have to struggle to teach in the three public universities that were available when we were young.
Kwadwo:	I fear for the future of Ghana's young private university system. The National Accreditation Board (NAB) must do more to ensure quality. There is a lot of apathy and indiscipline in the system and its affording some sub-par universities opportunities to make money at the expense of delivering quality education.
Kofi:	Why so?

Ghana has huge backlog of university aspirants which is a hangover from the days of exclusive public university. Despite the expansion in the existing public education system and several new private universities, demand from regional countries such as Nigeria and Ghana's growing population has resulted in inelastic demand for university education. Although there are new private universities now, the historically low graduate enrollment ratios and the fact that there were only three universities for the first 40 years of statehood means demand for university education far outstrips supply resulting in excess demand.

This excess demand for university education has resulted in the situation where potential students are focusing on access to education and are not picky about the quality. Some private universities are taking advantage of the situation and enrolling huge numbers of students some of whom are not qualified just to make money.

Kofi: Are you saying the students don't care that these universities are not of the best quality.

Kwadwo: Guess what, a student said when I posed the same question to her. I asked her if she was not concerned about the quality of the private university she was attending as there were rumors that the university was only employing part-time lecturers.

Kofi: Enye hwee.

Kwadwo: Exactly. She explained that she was interested in the degree not how quality the degree was.

After reading the stories in this chapter, it is natural to ask what the literature tells us about the relationship between corruption and culture. How can we take advantage of this knowledge to reduce any undesirable effects of corruption even if we cannot eliminate corruption altogether? I now present a review of the literature on corruption and culture.

What the Literature Says About Corruption and Culture

Despite some limited contributions in the development economics literature about the positive role of corruption in stimulating economic growth (see, e.g., Leff 1964; Kaufmann 1997; Huntington 2000; Beck and Maher 1986; Lien 1986), the pernicious effects of corruption on growth and development are well known (Krueger 1974; Baumol 1990; Murphy et al. 1991; Kaufmann and Wei 1999; World Bank 1993; Treisman 2000; Sandholtz and Taagepera 2005; Fisman and Gatti 2002; Dreher et al. 2007; Rose-Ackerman 1978, 1999, 2004; Tanzi 1998; Kofi Annan 2004; Klitgaard 1988; Smith 2007; Lipset and Lenz 2000; Bontis and Seleim 2009; Husted 1999; Barr and Sera 2010; Greif and Tabellini 2010;

Taras et al. 2010; Fisman and Miguel 2007, Yeganeh 2013; Tong 2014; Achim 2016; Klitgaard 2017; Lanier and Kirshner 2018; Ahmed 2018; Valdavinos 2019).

In the international context, trans-national institutions and whole governments have been brought to their knees because of corruption as in the case of the United State company, Enron (CNN 2019; Segal 2019). Governments in different parts of the world had been toppled, or replaced, through legal elections because of accusations of corruption. Several examples exist in Latin America. For example, in 2016, Odebrecht, a Brazilian construction company, paid over 800 million USD in bribes to different governments in Latin America leading to political upheaval in that region (Ahmed 2018; Valdavinos 2019).

In the first eight months of 2019, the Cable News Network (CNN) and Aljazeera run almost daily reports of political unrest in Venezuela, where incumbent, socialist President Nicholas Maduro is accused of significant corruption in managing the country's oil wealth. That country, besieged by economic recession, now has two sitting and opposing presidents concurrently in office. This is because opposition leader Juan Guaidó has also declared himself president with the backing of Western countries such as the United States of America.

Examples of corruption-induced conflict in North Africa and the Arab World include the Arab Spring that started in Tunisia and Spread to Egypt, Libya, Bahrain, Yemen and Algeria. According to a 2011 British Broadcasting Corporation (BBC) report by Frank Gardner, the Arab Spring started when a Tunisian citizen, Mohamed Bouazizi, was banned from selling fruit on the street, set himself on fire in protest of government corruption. All of Tunisia took notice and supported him, coming out in demonstrations calling for Tunisia's autocratic president, Zine al-Abidine Ben Ali, to resign. A month later, after 23 years in power, Ben Ali fled to Saudi Arabia (Gardner 2011).

The Arab Spring moved on to Egypt and removed long-serving Egyptian dictator Hosni Mubarak from power, then to Libya where it removed perennial Libyan Head of State Col. Muammar Gaddafi from power. More recently leaders like Algeria's Bouteflika and Omar Bashir of Sudan have also been deposed, accused of unspeakable acts of corruption (BBC 2018).

The Arab Spring also caused ongoing and damaging conflict in Syria and Yemen with associated atrocities committed by the warring factions and the onset of the world's worst case of cholera and concentrated poverty in Yemen (BBC, June 13, 2018).

According to BBC reports, in SSA, President Yahya Jammeh of the Gambia Jacob Zumah of South Africa and Robert Mugabe of Zimbabwe were removed from power respectively in 2017, 2018 and 2019 after several years of tyrannical rule because they were accused of committing very serious acts of corruption (CNN).

Even in Ghana, West Africa's most peaceful country and one of Africa's most democratic and peaceful countries (CNN), several governments have been removed in the past, on the accusation of corruption.

Given that the underlying factors responsible for stimulating and sustaining corruption may not generalize across different institutions, cultures and countries (Lanier and Kirshner 2018; Valdavinos 2019; Klitgaard 2017; Achim 2016; Tong 2014; McLaughlin 2013; Shadabi 2013; Lopez-Claros and Perotti 2014; Taras et al. 2010; Barr and Serra 2010; Fisman and Miguel 2007; Murdoch 2009; Halkos and Tzeremes 2011; Husted 1999; Granato et al. 1996; Bontis and Seleim 2009; Murdoch 2009; Davis and Ruhe 2003; Hofstede 1980, 2001; Hofstede et al. 2005; Hofstede and Minkov 2007, 2011; Schwartz 1999; Inglehart and Baker 2000; Landes 2000; Huntington 2000; Harrison and Huntington 2000), it is vital, in the Ghanaian context, to explain the determinants of corruption.

A deep appreciation of the cultural underpinning of corruption will help to combat corruption, or at least minimize its dire consequences (Hasty 2005). This will also help in to realize current Ghanaian president Nana Addo's vision of "Ghana beyond Aid": A self-reliant Ghana thriving on trade not aid.

In conceptualizing corruption, and formulating theories to analyze corruption, however, the economic development literature, until recently, ignored possible inter-relationships between corruption, culture, and development mainly because of a dearth of data (Granato et al. 1996; Alesina and Giuliano 2015), as well as definitional and measurement problems associated with respectively, the concepts of development (Amartya Sen 1999), corruption (Rose-Ackerman 1999) and culture (Alesina and Giuliano 2015, Tabellini 2010; Guiso et al. 2006).

After recognizing that the neoliberal, physical capital-driven model of Solow (1956), Swan (1956); Cass (1965), Koopmans (1965), Harrod (1939), Domar (1946) and Arthur Lewis (1954), supplemented by the new endogenous theory championed by, among others, Romer (1986, 1990),

Lucas (1988), Barro (1991), Barro and Lee (2001), Mankiw, Romer and Weil (1992) and Islam (1995) based on human capital accumulation (Schultz 1960; Becker 1964; Bowman 1966) did not quite effectively capture the growth experience of developing countries, nor explain the role of important determinants like corruption, the development economics literature for the past couple of decades has focused on strong, inclusive or effective institutions as the main determinant of economic development and for reducing corruption. I think qualifications are needed given the cultural context.

Except for the peculiar positive correlation between corruption and wealth found by Gatti et al. (2003), and Leff's (1964) claim that corruption enhances development by reducing transaction costs in bureaucratic economies, the overwhelming literature evidence supports the notion that income growth and development undermine the incentives for corruption (Bontis and Seleim 2009; Husted 1999; Achim 2016).

The shift of the development literature from reference to neoclassical determinants of growth particularly physical capital (Solow 1956; Swan 1956; Cass 1965; Harrod 1939; Domar 1946 and Arthur Lewis 1954) and technology-related arguments in the tradition of endogenous growth theory (Romer 1986, 1990; Lucas 1988; Barro 1991; Barro and Lee (2001; Mankiw et al. 1992 and Islam 1995) based on human capital accumulation (Schultz 1960; Becker 1964; Bowman 1966) to institutions as the key determinant of growth and corruption followed the seminal work of Acemoglu, Johnson and Robinson (2001) in an affirmation of Nobel winner Douglas North's (1990, 1991) thesis that the key factor in the development struggle is the strength of institutions.

Interestingly, Jeffrey Sachs's (2001) feeble protests to re-introduce geography and culture into the debate about the determinants of corruption and growth did not initially gain much traction in the literature. Despite the dominance of new institutional economics that claims that the key factor is institutions, the effects of some cultural variables on corruption, such as trust, was well known (see Banfield 1958; Arrow 1972; Putnam 1993; Fukuyama 1995). However, trust is often characterized as an institutional, not a cultural, variable.

Max Weber had documented "work-ethic" as a "Protestant cultural trait" responsible for the success of protestant compared to catholic Europe in his work on the *Protestant Ethic*. However, he seemed to have overlooked acknowledging the contribution of Chinese philosopher

Confucius's work, several millennia before him detailing a Sino-based work ethic (Granato et al. 1996; Weber 1976).

According to Sandholtz and Taagepera (2005), consistent with Webber, Protestantism is positively related to growth and development and negatively correlated with corruption in some studies (Sandholtz and Koetzle 2000; Treisman 2000). However, this significance is lost with larger sample sizes and additional controls (Sandholtz and Gray 2003).

Another cultural determinant of corruption: the loyalty to in-family as opposed to non-family members, akin to the mafia in Italy (Lipset and Lenz 2000; Greif 1994, Greif 2006a, b, Algan and Cahuc 2014; Greif and Tabellini 2010; Banfield 1958), was well researched.

Non-cultural variables that were known to influence corruption included the discretionary power of government officials in bureaucratic societies (Kaufmann 1997; Bardhan 1997; Ampratwum 1987) the effect of income, which was found to be negatively correlated with corruption (Mauro 1995; Bontis and Seleim 2009; Ades and Di Tella 1999; Sandholtz and Koetzle 2000; Treisman 2000) and foreign aid which was found to be a corrupting influence on development (Moyo 2009).

Other variables correlated with corruption include Gender (Swamy et al. 2001; Dollar et al. 2001; Alatas et al. 2009; Fernández and Fogli 2009) and age (Gatti et al. 2003). However, gender and age were considered social variables that affected corruption and were considered somewhat outside the cultural effect with women being less corrupt than men and the aged less corrupt than the youth.

However, possible interactions between corruption and different dimensions of culture were largely unexplored prior to Hofstede's (1980) seminal article categorizing culture into measurable variables. Following the work by Geert Hofstede (1980), Shalom Schwartz (1988, 1999), Hofstede et al. (2010), Minkov (2007, 2011) and Ronald Inglehart (2000) among others to categorize culture into different dimensions, an active research agenda has surfaced to try to explain the relationships if any between the dimensions of culture as defined by Hofstede and corruption. According to Achim (2016), Hofstede's cultural model has six dimensions. The first four were introduced before the last two were introduced later. The six dimensions are:

1. Attitude toward social inequality or power distance (PD)
2. Attitude toward the community or individualism versus collectivism (IDV)

3. Attitude toward success or masculinity versus femininity (MAS)
4. Attitude toward the unknown or uncertainty avoidance (UA)
5. Attitude toward the passage of time or long-term orientation (LTO)
6. Attitude toward control of one's own desires or indulgence and restraint (IND)

Each dimension places the culture of a nation on a scale from 0 to 100 with 100 representing the stronger effect. Hofstede's model was applied to 100 countries (Hofstede Centre 2015). Using data on the different dimensions of culture identified by Hofstede, Husted (1999) finds that some of the dimensions of culture defined by Hofstede (1980, 1990) were significantly related to corruption.

According to Husted (1999) the cultural profile of a corrupt country is one in which there are high power distance (PD), high masculinity (MASC) and high Uncertainty Avoidance (UA). Bontis and Seleim (2009) reach similar conclusion to Husted (1999) with a few differences. They find empirical support for the influence of individual versus collectivism, uncertainty avoidance values and human orientation practices by trying to use the Global Leadership and Organizational Behavior Effectiveness (GLOBE) data set to confirm Husted's (1999) findings. Various studies document a positive relationship between power distance (PD) and corruption (Husted 1999; Davis and Ruhe 2003; Murdoch 2009; Halkos and Tzeremes 2011; McLaughlin 2013; Tong 2014).

According to Husted, what motivated his work was that available empirical literature consists of single-country case studies of corruption (Bunker and Cohen 1983; Dombrink 1988; Wade 1985). Other work investigated perceptions of businesspeople or students of corrupt practices in one or more countries.

Clearly the available literature ignored the possible relationship between culture and corruption, and it does not explain why corruption varies across nations so the usefulness is limited. This is why Husted (1999) investigated the effect of Hofstede's cultural dimensions on perception of corruption.

Fisman and Miguel (2007) investigated the relationship between culture and corruption by conducting a survey of New York's parking violations by diplomats from over 149 countries. They found out that diplomats from highly corrupt countries are more likely to violate parking law than diplomats from less corrupt countries. They concluded that corruption is partially a cultural phenomenon.

The experimental economics literature has also analyzed the effect of culture on corruption. They reach the same conclusion regarding culture's effect on corruption as reached by Fisman and Miguel (2007). Specifically, in 2005 and 2007, Barr and Serra (2010) conducted two experiments on bribery, with Oxford University students participating as subjects who belong to some of the most and least corrupt countries in the world, 33 and 22 countries in total, respectively. Both experiments revealed that among undergraduates, culture significantly influences corruption, but the reverse is the case for graduates. Thus, the values and beliefs toward corruption may be strongly related to the country of origin and the associated culture of the country.

Ronal Inglehart, an originator of the World Values Survey (WVS) data, which is the alternative database to Hofstede for cultural data, is a key figure in the literature trying to identify the relationships between culture development and corruption. This more recent literature with contributions from Harrison and Huntington (2000); Huntington (2000), Landes (2000), Fukuyama (1995), Getz and Volkema (2001), Davis and Ruhe (2003), Alatas et al. (2009), Sandholtz and Taagepera (2005), Daniel Jordan Smith (2007), Lipset and Lenz (2000), Bontis and Seleim (2009), Husted (1999), Barr and Sera (2010), Greif and Tabellini (2010), Taras et al. (2010), Fisman and Miguel (2007), Yeganeh (2013), Tong (2014), Achim (2016), Klitgaard (2017) and Lanier and Kirshner (2018) seems to agree with Harrison and Huntington (2000) that "culture matters" and with Landes (2000) that indeed "culture makes all the difference."

Lanier and Kirshner (2018) summed up what was known in the literature until their work by coming up with a parsimonious empirical model for investigating the effect of corruption on culture. The model reflected the importance of long-term orientation (LTO) as a key cultural variable once it was interacted with indulgence and constraint variables.

This is key because Minkov (2011) reports that he only updated the dataset containing Hofstede's four original cultural dimensions (power distance, collectivism versus individualism, uncertainty avoidance and masculinity versus femininity) in 2010 jointly with Geert Hofstede and his eldest son Gert Hofstede. This means work before 2010 likely did not include the two cultural variables later incorporated into Hofstede's cultural dimensions: indulgence versus restraint (INDR) and long-term (LTO) versus short-term orientation of time.

Incidentally, LTO seems to capture all the cultural variables that Huntington (2000) described as important for explaining Korea's superior development compared to Ghana: discipline, investment, organization, hard work, thrift and education (Heffner 2002). The exclusion of LTO historically and the subsequent inclusion therefore seems to place heavier weight on research results post inclusion of the LTO variables at least for the case of Ghana following Huntington's observations.

However, Valdovinos et al. (2019) in trying to replicate the empirical literature conclusions about the effects of Hofstede's cultural dimensions on culture as conducted by Husted (1999) and Bontis and Seleim (2009) found contradicting results for some of the key cultural variables. Clearly, the literature has not come to consensus about the impact of culture on corruption, but it seems naive to ignore culture in strategizing for Ghanaian development given how important culture is to the Ghanaian in Ghanaian development discourse.

Confronting Corruption in the Cultural Context: What to Do?

The illustration provided by the short stories of how culture and corruption interact in Ghana and the review of the literature on culture and corruption seems to support Huntington's (2000) assertion that "culture matters" and that "Culture makes all the difference" as emphasized by Landes (2000).

The development economics literature is correct to take a second look at culture in formulating more effective development strategy given the apparent impotency of development advice to developing countries thus far. The complexity of the corruption-culture interaction is based on a particular "programming of the mind" as Hofstede (1980) puts it that incentives a person to consider whether or not to commit to the type of action which in Rose-Ackerman's (1978) words will constitute an "abuse of the public trust for private gain" or corruption.

The interaction between culture and corruption may also explain, at least in part, why SSA has struggled so much with corruption and development in general. Common culture tends to unite people. However, when very distinct people with very different cultures, languages, values and beliefs live closely together in very close proximity as is often seen in an African country like Ghana, the cultural difference can be a source of conflict not progress if not managed properly.

It is perhaps not also surprising that, Botswana, one of the few African countries that have succeeded in growing consistently in its entire post-independence period, is one of the least heterogeneous countries in Africa as it is dominated by one tribe, the Twa.

Botswana has been one of the fastest-growing countries in the world for the last 50 years and was slowed down only by an HIV epidemic in the 1990s and the recent global financial crises although it seems to have recovered.

According to Acemoglu, Johnson and Robinson (2001), Botswana is dominated by the Twa tribe whose institutions were inclusive and served as the basis of the strong institutions that propelled Botswana to development. Botswana has grown consistently despite an adverse geography and a small population but of course with help from the revenue derived from a significant endowment of diamonds.

So why is Botswana enjoying a resource blessing while other African countries like the Congo, Liberia, Sierra Leone, Nigeria and even Ghana that are also endowed with natural resources not doing well. These countries vary in population size from small to large, so it is probably not Botswana's low population that is the reason for their better performance. Acemoglu and Johnson explain that the reason why Botswana performs well is its strong institutions.

Even if we were to accept that Botswana's strong economic performance is due to its strong institutions, where did these strong institutions come from? It is reasonable to surmise that Botswana's strong institutions came out from the culture of a "more or less" homogenous people under the guidance of strong effective non-corrupt leaders. The evidence bears this out: Botswana's leaders have been consistently adjudged as among the best in Africa by the Mo Ibrahim index.

When different cultures exist in a melting pot such as is found in Congo, Ghana and Nigeria, the diversity of the people, made up of historically different nation-states, living within the same nation, artificially constituted by Europeans, but with rights to a common resources, does not bode well for peace. The diversity must be managed by strong effective leaders who may or may not emerge.

An obvious follow-up question is why did leaders of integrity who were ready to the right thing emerge in Botswana but not the other African countries including Ghana? One answer is that the assertion that leaders did not emerge in Ghana, Nigeria and Congo is, itself, presumptive. Ghana produced Kwame Nkrumah, Nigeria produced Obafemi Awolowo and Congo produced Patrice Lumumba, all of whom were visionary leaders.

However, the different tribal or ethnic makeup of these African countries made them susceptible to divide-and-conquer tactics first by their colonizers and subsequently by Western powers with designs on African resources to fuel their own economies. The SSA countries were not united under strong leadership. However, it seems the one sure way to fight corruption is unity under strong leadership that is visionary and incorruptible.

Yes, it is impressive that the leaders in Botswana such as Ian Khama and later Seretse Khama among others ruled the country well. In some cases, they took decisions that were not aligned with their own interest but in the interest of the people. They essentially overcame the principal agent problem identified in the context of developing countries by Acemoglu, Johnson and Robinson (2001). For example, they lowered their own powers and the ability to commit corrupt acts as the executive, when they created the independent special prosecutor to prosecute politically exposed persons. This is largely absent in African countries with non-homogenous populations where the rulers intend to use the political power either for private gain or to advance the status of their tribes.

To reduce corruption and grow, the first challenge that confronts African leaders is to unite their people. The African leaders that have tried to do so like Paul Kagame of Rwanda have had reasonable success. Kagame inherited a country that had gone through an ethnic-based genocide. However, by focusing on the country instead of tribes and leading with integrity, Kagame has transformed Rwanda into one of the least corrupt and attractive places to do business.

In contrast, Botswana has performed very well but did not have to spend much energy to unite because they were mainly homogenous and did have progressive traditional values and strong leaders that translated into strong institutions.

Unfortunately, almost all of Africa's leaders seem to be heeding Kwame Nkrumah's now infamous advice, "Seek ye first the political kingdom and everything else shall be added unto you." In typical Machiavellian fashion, these SSA country leaders seem to want to hang on to power by any means necessary. Such a mindset of course is not supportive of development as such leaders will have to subvert the will of the people to achieve their agenda.

The frightening extent of diversity in SSA countries that Europeans took advantage of to perpetuate the slave trade and colonization of Africa is probably one of the main reasons for Africa's disunity and created the conditions for mis-governance.

This diversity can easily lead to a Mafioso like dispensation of tribal politics where people support their tribesmen who are in power and will not hold them to account for any wrongdoing leading to corrupt practices. Colonization and the Slave Trade also led to even more distrust and disunity among neighboring tribes in the same nation, presenting very difficult challenges of governance to the new African nations (Bates 2006).

Despite the challenges I have described that face African countries, I am in no way trying to make excuses for them. Africa should have done and must do better in promoting development and reducing corruption.

I do support in part, the well-meaning advice that President Obama gave to Africans when he visited Ghana in July 2009, that "African countries need strong institutions not strong leaders." Although Obama should have revealed that such an advice was well documented in the literature by Acemoglu, Johnson and Robinson (2001) instead of trying to pass it off as his own, it is good advice. I only support it in part because African countries need not only strong institutions but also effective leaders. Strong institutions will not emerge out of thin air. It will take effective and courageous or "strong leaders" to change mindsets and, in some cases, change aspects of the culture of the people to establish strong institutions.

I must confess here that I am underwhelmed by what appears to be the consensus in the literature on corruption and culture about how to deal with aspects of the culture of a people that support corruption and undermine development. For example, Klitgaard (2017), a renowned expert on the study of culture, suggests it may be counterproductive to change aspects of people's culture. Instead strategies that change the incentives underlying corrupt behavior but leave the culture unchanged are preferable especially since culture is difficult to change.

Lanier and Kirshner (2018) seems to agree with Klitgaard (2017). He suggests that strategies that accommodate the culture of a people have a better chance at succeeding than attempting to change the culture of a people because culture is difficult to change.

The problem with the suggested strategies to combat corruption in the corruption-culture literature is that the aspects of culture of a people that support corruption may be linked to the mindset of the people. If that is indeed the case, how can one hope to reduce corruption without changing mindsets? The problem is a difficult one, but reducing the scale of the problem will not give an effective solution. Culture is difficult to change but to get results, we must work to change culture that is perverse. Accommodating indolence, indiscipline and tardiness is not an option.

Hofstede defined culture as "the programming of the mind that distinguishes one group of people from another" (Hofstede 1980). Evaluating Huntington's (2000) suggestions that the differential performance of Ghana's economy compared to South Korea was due to differences in culture ["while South Koreans valued thrift, investment, hard work, education, organization, and discipline, Ghanaians had different values" (Huntington 2000)] could well lead an objective reader to conclude that the challenge Ghanaians have is a "mindset problem." In such a case trying to stop corruption while running away from the deeper problem of changing mindsets just constitutes kicking the can further down the road. Nothing will change.

The author contends that the assertion that only strategies consistent with current cultures or that accommodate current existing culture are effective in foiling corruption or spurring growth, although well intentioned and cautionary in approach, will achieve little in terms of preventing, reducing or eliminating corruption.

It may be the case that the authors in the corruption-culture literature only intend to point to the difficulty of the problem of changing aspects of a culture. Maybe, they do not want to disturb established age-old African practices, values and beliefs for the sake of political correctness. I disagree with that approach.

I think Africa and specifically Ghana deserves better than that. How much impact can be made on reducing corruption and promoting growth if we were to accommodate a culture that in Huntington's (2000) words does not value "thrift, discipline, hard work, savings, organization and education." Difficult as it is, it must be done.

I think authors like Klitgaard and Lanier in their cautionary approach ignore the potential for education, inspirational leadership with integrity, and the use of technology to change mindsets. At least one examples of such a positive change that I know of in Africa exist and offers useful lessons.

Bibliography

Acemoglu, D., Johnson, S., & Robinson, J. A. (2001). The Colonial Origins of Comparative Development: An Empirical Investigation. *American Economic Review, 91*, 1369–1401.

Achim, M. V. (2016). Cultural Dimension of Corruption: A Cross-Country Survey. *International Advances in Economic Research, 22*, 333–345.

Ades, A., & Di Tella, R. (1999). Rents, Competition, and Corruption. *American Economic Review, 89*(4), 982–993.

Ahmed, A. (2018). Criminal Cases in Graft Scandal Stifled in Mexico – Mexico Could Press Bribery Charges. It Just Hasn't. *The New York Times*, p. A1. Available at https://www.nytimes.com/2018/06/11/world/americas/mexico-odebrecht-investigation.html

Alatas, et al. (2009, January). Gender, Culture, and Corruption: Insights from an Experimental Analysis. *Southern Economic Journal, 75*(3), 663–680.

Alesina, A., & Giuliano, P. (2015). Culture and Institutions. *Journal of Economic Literature, 53*(4), 898–944.

Algan, Y., & Cahuc, P. (2014). Trust, Growth, and Well-Being: New Evidence and Policy Implications. In P. Aghion & S. N. Durlauf (Eds.), *Handbook of Economic Growth* (Vol. 2A, pp. 49–120). Amsterdam/San Diego: Elsevier, North-Holland.

Ampratwum, E. F. (1987). The Fight Against Corruption and its Implications for Development in Developing and Transition Economies. *Journal of Money Laundering Control, 11*(1), 76–87.

Annan, K. (2004). *Statement by the Secretary General on the Adoption by the General Assembly of the United Nations (UN) Convention Against Corruption*. New York: The United Nations Office on Drugs and Crime (UNODOC).

Armah, S. E. (2016). Strategies to Stimulate Ghana's Economic Transformation and Diversification. *Ashesi Economics Lecture Series Journal, 2*(1), 9–16.

Arrow, K. J. (1972). Gifts and Exchanges. *Philosophy & Public Affairs, 1*, 343–362.

Aryeetey, E., & Kanbur, R. (2016). *The Economy of Ghana Sixty Years After Independence*. Oxford: Oxford University Press.

Banerjee, A. (1999). A Theory of Misgovernance. *Quarterly Journal of Economics, 112*(4), 1289–1332. 1997.

Banfield, E. (1958). *The Moral Basis of a Backward Society*. New York: Simon and Schuster.

Banfield, E. C. (1985). Corruption as a Feature of Governmental Organization. In *Here the People Rule* (pp. 147–170). Boston: Springer.

Bardhan, P. (1997). Corruption and Development: A Review of Issues. *Journal of Economic Literature, 35*, 1320–1346.

Barr, A., & Serra, D. (2010). Corruption and Culture: An Experimental Analysis. *Journal of Public Economics, 94*, 862–869.

Barro, R. J. (1991, May). Economic Growth in a Cross Section of Countries. *Quarterly Journal of Economics, 106*(2), 407–443.

Barro, R., & Lee, J.-W. (2001). International Data on Educational Attainment: Updates and Implications. *Oxford Economic Papers, 3*, 541–563.

Bates, R. H. (2006). Institutions and Development. *Journal of African Economies, 15*(Suppl. 1), 10–61.

Baumol, W. (1990). Entrepreneurship: Productive, Unproductive and Destructive. *The Journal of Political Economy, 98*(5), 893–921.

Beck, P. J., & Maher, M. W. (1986). A Comparison of Bribery and Bidding in Thin Markets. *Economics Letters, 20*(1), 1–5.

Becker, G. (1964). *Human Capital: A Theoretical and Empirical Analysis, with Special Reference to Education*. New York: National Bureau of Economic Research.

Becker, G. S., & Stigler, G. J. (1974). Law Enforcement, Malfeasance, and Compensation of Enforcers. *The Journal of Legal Studies, 3*(1), 1–18.

Bontis, N., & Seleim, A. (2009). The Relationship between Culture and Corruption: A Cross-National Study. *Journal of Intellectual Capital, 10*(1), 165–184. https://doi.org/10.1108/14691930910922978.

Bowman, M. (1966). The Human Investment Revolution in Economic Thought. *Sociology of Education, 39*(2), 111. https://doi.org/10.2307/2111863.

British Broadcasting Corporation (BBC). (2018). *The Yemen Crisis in 400 words*. https://www.bbc.com/news/world-middle-east-44466574

Burbach, T. (2016, September 22). *The Coming Peace: Africa's Declining Conflicts, Oxford Research Group*. https://www.oxfordresearchgroup.org.uk/blog/the-coming-peace-africas-declining-conflicts

Cable News Network (CNN). (2019, April). *Enron Fast Facts. CNN Library*. https://edition.cnn.com/2013/07/02/us/enron-fast-facts/index.html

Cass, D. (1965). Optimum Growth in an Aggregative Model of Capital Accumulation. *Review of Economic Studies, 32*, 233–240.

Davis, J. H., & Ruhe, J. A. (2003). Perceptions of Country Corruption: Antecedents and Outcomes. *Journal of Business Ethics, 43*(4), 275–288.

Dollar, D., Fisman, R., & Gatti, R. (2001). Are Women Really the "Fairer" Sex? Corruption and Women in Government. *Journal of Economic Behavior and Organization, 46*(4), 423–429.

Domar, E. (1946). Capital Expansion, Rate of Growth and Employment. *Econometrica, 14*(2), 137–147. https://doi.org/10.2307/1905364. JSTOR 1905364.

Dreher, A., Kotsogiannis, C., & McCorriston, S. (2007). Corruption Around the World: Evidence from a Structural Model. *Journal of Comparative Economics, 35*, 443–466.

Fernández, R., & Fogli, A. (2009). Culture: An Empirical Investigation of Beliefs, Work, and Fertility. *American Economic Journal: Macroeconomics, 1*(1), 146–177.

Fisman, R., & Gatti, R. (2002). Decentralization and Corruption: Evidence Across Countries. *Journal of Public Economics, 83*(2002), 325–345.

Fisman, R., & Miguel, E. (2007). Corruption, Norms, and Legal Enforcement: Evidence from Diplomatic Parking Tickets. *Journal of Political Economy, 115*(6), 1020–1048.

Fukuyama, F. (1995). *Trust: The Social Virtues and the Creation of Prosperity* (Vol. 99). New York: Free Press.

Gardner, F. (2011). How the Arab Spring Begun. *The BBC.* https://www.bbc.com/news/av/world-middle-east-16212447/how-the-arab-spring-began

Gatti, R., Paternostro, S., & Rigolini, J. (2003, August). Individual Attitudes Toward Corruption: Do Social Effects Matter? (World Bank Policy Research Working Paper 3122).

Getz, K. A., & Volkema, R. J. (2001). Culture, Perceived Corruption, and Economics. *Business and Society, 40*(1), 7–31.

Ghanaweb. (2018). *Woyome Settles ¢4.6m of ¢51m Debt.* https://www.ghanaweb.com/GhanaHomePage/NewsArchive/Woyome-settles-4-6m-of-51m-debt-676381

Ghanaweb. (2019, September 16). Apologize to Ghanaians for Dashing Bauxite to Your Brother – NPP Tells Mahama. *Ghanaweb.* https://www.ghanaweb.com/GhanaHomePage/NewsArchive/Apologize-to-Ghanaians-for-dashing-bauxite-to-your-brother-NPP-tells-Mahama-781362

Glynn, P., Kobrin, S. J., & Naim, M. (1997). The Globalization of Corruption. *Corruption and the Global Economy, 7,* 17.

Gould, D. J. (1991). Administrative Corruption: Incidence, Causes and Remedial Strategies. In A. Farazmand (Ed.), *Handbook of Comparative and Development Public Administration.* New York: Marcel Dekker.

Granato, J., Inglehart, R., & Leblang, D. (1996). The Effect of Cultural Values on Economic Development: Theory, Hypotheses, and Some Empirical Tests. *American Journal of Political Science, 40,* 607–631.

Greif, A. (1994). Cultural Beliefs and the Organization of Society: A Historical and Theoretical Reflection on Collectivist and Individualist Societies. *Journal of Political Economy, 102*(5), 912–950.

Greif, A. (2006a). Family Structure, Institutions, and Growth: The Origins and Implications of Western Corporations. *American Economic Review, 96*(2), 308–312.

Greif, A. (2006b). *Institutions and the Path to the Modern Economy: Lessons from Medieval Trade.* Cambridge: Cambridge University Press.

Greif, A., & Tabellini, G. (2010). Cultural and Institutional Bifurcation: China and Europe Compared. *American Economic Review, 100*(2), 135–140.

Guiso, L., Sapienza, P., & Zingales, L. (2006). Does Culture Affect Economic Outcomes? *Journal of Economic Perspectives, 20*(2), 23–48.

Guiso, L., Sapienza, P., & Zingales, L. (2015). Corporate Culture, Societal Culture, and Institutions. *American Economic Review, 105*(5), 336–339.

Halkos, G. E., & Tzeremes N. G. (2011). *Investigating the Cultural Patterns of Corruption: A Nonparametric Analysis*. MPRA Munich Personal RePEc Archive.

Harrison, L. E., & Huntington, S. P. (Eds.). (2000). *Culture Matters: How Values Shape Human Progress*. New York: Basic Books.

Harrod, R. F. (1939). An Essay in Dynamic Theory. *The Economic Journal, 49*(193), 14–33. https://doi.org/10.2307/2225181. JSTOR 2225181.

Hasty, J. (2005). The Pleasures of Corruption: Desire and Discipline in Ghanaian Political Culture. *Cultural Anthropology, 20*(2), 271–301.

Heffner, F. (2002). The Role of Beliefs and Cultural Attitudes in Economic Development. *The Review of Regional Studies, 32*(1), 1–8.

Herald. (2018, November 1). *Maritime Boss Fixes 11 Air-Conditioners in Gov't Bungalow*. http://theheraldghana.com/maritime-boss-fixes-11-air-conditioners-in-govt-bungalow/

Hofstede, G. (1980). *Culture's Consequences: International Differences in Work-Related Values*. Beverly Hills: Sage Publishers.

Hofstede, G. (1990). *Cultures and Organizations: Software of the Mind*. London: McGraw-Hill.

Hofstede, G. (2001). *Culture's Consequences: Comparing Values, Behaviours, Institutions, and Organizations Across Nations* (2nd ed.). Thousand Oaks: Sage.

Hofstede, G., Hofstede, G. J., & Minkov, M. (2005). *Cultures and Organizations: Software of the Mind* (Vol. 2). New York: McGraw-Hill.

Hofstede, G., Hofstede, G. J., & Minkov, M. (2010). *Cultures & Organizations: Software of the Mind*. New York: McGraw.

Huntington, S. (2000). *Political Order in Changing Societies*. New Haven: Yale University Press.

Husted, B. (1999). Corruption and Culture. *Journal of International Business Studies, 30*(2), 339. 2nd Qtr.

Inglehart, R., & Baker, W. E. (2000). Modernization, Cultural Change, and the Persistence of Traditional Values. *American Sociological Review, 65*(1), 19–51.

Islam, N. (1995). Growth Empirics: A Panel Data Approach. *Quarterly Journal of Economics, 110*, 1127–1170.

Kaufmann, D. (1997). *Corruption: The Facts* (pp. 114–131). Available at www.Jstor.org/. Accessed 13 Nov 2006.

Kaufmann, D., & Wei, S. J. (1999). *Does "Grease Money" Speed Up the Wheels of Commerce?* (No. w7093). National Bureau of Economic Research.

Klitgaard, R. (1988). *Controlling Corruption*. Berkeley/Los Angeles: University of California Press.

Klitgaard, R. (1991). *Controlling Corruption*. Berkeley/Los Angeles: University of California Press.

Klitgaard, R. (2017, June 13). *On Corruption and Culture*. Paper Presented at the Public Integrity and Anti-Corruption Workshop at Nuffield College, Oxford.

Koopmans, T. C. (1965). On the Concept of Optimal Economic Growth. In *(Study Week on the) Econometric Approach to Development Planning, Chapter 4* (pp. 225–287). Amsterdam: North-Holland Publishing.

Krueger, A. O. (1974). The Political Economy of the Rent-Seeking Society. *The American Economic Review, 64*(3), 291–303.

Landes, D. (2000). Culture Makes Almost All the Difference. In *Culture Matters: How Values Shape Human Progress* (pp. 2–13). New York: Basic Books.

Lanier, C., & Kirshner, M. (2018). Corruption and Culture: Empirical Analysis of Long-Term Indulgence and Corrupt Systems. *The Review of Business, and Interdisciplinary Journal on Risk and Society, 38*(2), 30–43.

Leff, N. H. (1964). Economic Development Through Bureaucratic Corruption. *American Behavioral Scientist, 8*(3), 8–14.

Lewis, W. A. (1954). Econ Development with Unlimited Supplies of Labor. *The Manchester School of Economic and Social Studies, 22*, 139–192.

Lien, D. H. D. (1986). A Note on Competitive Bribery Games. *Economics Letters, 22*(4), 337–341.

Lipset, S. M., & Lenz, G. S. (2000). Corruption, Culture, and Markets. In L. E. Harrison & S. P. Huntington (Eds.), *Culture Matters: How Values Shape Human Progress* (pp. 112–125). New York: Basic Books.

Lopez-Claros, A., & Perotti, V. (2014). *Does Culture Matter for Development?* Policy Research Working Paper No. WPS 7092. Washington, DC: World Bank Group.

Lucas, R. (1988). On the Mechanics of Economic Development. *Journal of Monetary Economics, 22*, 3–42.

Lucas, R. E., Jr. (1990). Why Doesn't Capital Flow from Rich to Poor Countries? *The American Economic Review, 80*(2), 92–96. Papers and Proceedings of the Hundred and Second Annual Meeting of the American Economic Association.

Manasseh, A. (2016, June). *Full Story: President Mahama's 'Gift' from Burkinabe Contractor.* http://www.manassehazure.com/2016/06/full-story-president-mahamas-gift-burkinabe-contractor/

Mankiw, N. G., Romer, D., & Weil, D. N. (1992, May). Contribution to the Empirics of Economic Growth. *The Quarterly Journal of Economics, 107*(2), 407–437.

Mauro, P. (1995). Corruption and Growth. *The Quarterly Journal of Economics, 110*(3), 681–712.

McLaughlin, E. (2013). Culture and Corruption: An Explanation of the Differences Between Scandinavia and Africa, American International Journal of Research in Humanities. *Arts and Social Sciences, 2*(2), 85–91.

Minkov, M. (2007). *What Makes Us Different and Similar: A New Interpretation of the World Values and Other Cross-Cultural Data.* Sofia: Klasika i Stil Publishing House.

Minkov, M. (2011). *Cultural Differences in a Globalizing World.* London: Emerald Group Publishing.

Murdoch, A. (2009). How Much Culture Is There in Corruption? Some Thoughts on Transformation-Cum-Collective Culture Shock in Post-Communist Poland. *Journal of Intercultural Management, 1*(1), 42–63.

Murphy, K. M., Shleifer, A., & Vishny, R. W. (1991). The Allocation of Talent: Implications for Growth. *The Quarterly Journal of Economics, 106*(2), 503–530.

Myjoyonline. (2018, June 28). *The 1979 Killing of Army Generals Unjustifiable; Activist 'Confesses' After 39 yrs.* https://www.myjoyonline.com/politics/2018/June-28th/1979-killing-of-army-generals-unjustifiable-activist-confesses-after-39yrs.php

Ndulu, B. J., & O'Connell, S. A. (2007). Policy Plus: African Economic Growth, 1960–2000 (Chapter 1). In B. J. Ndulu & S. A. O'Connell (Eds.), *The Political Economy of Economic Growth in Africa, 1960–2000*. Cambridge: Cambridge University Press.

North, D. (1990). *Institutions, Institutional Change, and Economic Performance*. New York: Cambridge University Press.

North, D. (1991). Institutions. *Journal of Economic Perspective, 5*(1), 97–112.

Nye, J. S. (1967). Corruption and Political Development: A Cost-Benefit Analysis. *American Political Science Review, 61*(2), 417–427.

Olken, B. A. (2007). Monitoring Corruption: Evidence from a Field Experiment in Indonesia. *Journal of Political Economy, 115*(2), 200–249.

Putnam, R. (1993). Explaining Institutional Performance. In *Making Democracy Work* (pp. 83–120). Princeton: Princeton University Press.

Romer, P. (1990). Human Capital and Growth: Theory and Evidence. *Carnegie Rochester Conference Series on Public Policy, 32*, 251–286.

Rose-Ackerman, S. (1975). The Economics of Corruption. *Journal of Public Economics, 4*(2), 187–203.

Rose-Ackerman, S. (1978). *Corruption: A Study of Political Economy*. New York: Academic Press.

Rose-Ackerman, S. (1999). *Corruption and Government*. Cambridge: Cambridge University Press.

Rose-Ackerman, S. (2004). *The Challenge of Poor Governance and Corruption*. Especial 1 DIREITO GV L. Rev., p. 207.

Sachs, J. D., & Warner, A. M. (2001). The Curse of Natural Resources. *European Economic Review, 45*(4–6), 827–838.

Sandholtz, W., & Gray, M. M. (2003). International Integration and National Corruption. *International Organization, 57*(4), 761–800.

Sandholtz, W., & Koetzle, W. (2000). Accounting for Corruption: Economic Structure, Democracy, and Trade. *International Studies Quarterly, 44*(1), 31–50.

Sandholtz, W., & Taagepera, R. (2005). Corruption, Culture, and Communism. *International Review of Sociology, 15*(1), 109–131.

Schleifer, A., & Vishny, R. W. (1993). Corruption. *Quarterly Journal of Economics, 108*(3), 599–617.

Schultz, T. W. (1960, December). Capital Formation by Education. *Journal of Political Economy, 68*, 571–583.

Schwartz, S. H. (1999). A Theory of Cultural Values and Some Implications for Work. *Applied Psychology, 48*(1), 23–47.

Segal, T. (2019, May). *The Enron Scandal. The Fall of a Wallstreet Darling.* Laws and Regulation; Crime and Fraud. https://www.investopedia.com/updates/enron-scandal-summary/

Sen, A. (1999). *Development as Freedom.* Oxford: Oxford University Press.

Shadabi, L. (2013). The Impact of Religion on Corruption. *The Journal of Business Inquiry, 12*, 102–117.

Smith, D. J. (2007). *A Culture of Corruption: Everyday Deception and Popular Discontent in Nigeria.* Princeton: Princeton University Press.

Solow. (1956). A Contribution to the Theory of Economic Growth. *Quarterly Journal of Economics, 70*(1), 65–94.

Straus, S. (2012). Wars Do End! Changing Patterns of Political Violence in Sub-Saharan Africa. *African Affairs, 111*(443), 179–201.

Strykker, R. (2019, September 9). Why 'Not Ghana Beyond Corruption' – Dutch Ambassador Asks. *Myjoyonline News.* https://www.myjoyonline.com/politics/2019/September-6th/why-not-ghana-beyond-corruption-dutch-ambassador-asks.php

Swamy, A., Knack, S., Lee, Y., & Azfar, O. (2001). Gender and Corruption. *Journal of Development Economics, 64*, 25–55.

Swan, T. (1956). Economic Growth and Capital Accumulation. *Economic Record, 32*(63), 334–361.

Tabellini, G. (2010). Culture and Institutions: Economic Development in the Regions of Europe. *Journal of the European Economic Association, 8*(4), 677–716.

Tanzi, V. (1998). Corruption Around the World: Causes, Consequences, Scope, and Cures. *Staff Papers, 45*(4), 559–594.

Taras, V., Kirkman, B. L., & Steel, P. (2010). Examining the Impact of Culture's Consequences: A Three-Decade, Multilevel, Meta-Analytic Review of Hofstede's Cultural Value Dimensions. *Journal of Applied Psychology, 95*(3), 405–439.

Tong, W. (2014). Analysis of Corruption from Sociocultural Perspectives. *International Journal of Business and Social Science, 5*(11), 1–19.

Treisman, D. (2000). The Causes of Corruption: A Cross-National Study. *Journal of Public Economics, 76*(3), 399–457.

Valdovinos, I. A., Szymanski, M., & Grabowska, K. (2019). Revisiting Corruption and Culture – Are there Really Cultures more Prone to Corruption? *Forum Scientiae Oeconomia, 7*(1), 103–120.

Waterbury, J. (1973). Endemic and Planned Corruption in a Monarchical Regime. *World Politics, 25*(4), 533–555.

Weber, M. (1976). *The Protestant Ethic and the Spirit of Capitalism.* London: George Allen & Unwin. [Original work published 1930].

Wiki. (2019). Death of Brigadier Emmauel Kwasi Kotoka. In Wikipedia. Assessed 5 Jan 2020.

World Bank. (1993). *The East Asian Miracle: Economic Growth and Public Policy* (pp. 611–638). Washington, DC/Dordrecht: World Bank Economics/Springer.

Yeganeh, H. (2013). *The Cultural Antecedents of Corruption: A Cross-National Study.* Quebec: International Conference of HEI: State Capitalism in the New Global Political Economy.

CHAPTER 5

Concluding Remarks

Abstract This chapter summarizes the lessons from Chaps. 1, 2, 3 and 4 and offers a conclusion. The chapter highlights the fact that instead of accommodating perverse cultures, or even designing strategies consistent with existing culture, an effective developmental strategy for African countries like Ghana must focus on changing mindsets, minimizing corruption, enhancing productivity and strengthening institutions as needed. A mindset change may be relevant even if it is contrary to established perverse culture that is supportive of corruption.

Keywords Developmental strategy • Institutions • Culture • Corruption and productivity

From the summary of the literature on culture and institutions, it is obvious Ghanaian policymakers will not transform and diversify Ghana's economy by avoiding cultural challenges. This is because not only culture matter in development as has been identified by Landes (2000) and Huntington (2000) culture is extremely important to the Ghanaian. The Ghanaian people will ignore leaders and policymakers who ignore culture condemning the policies of such well-meaning and knowledgeable economists or leaders to failure.

Chapters 1 and 2 identified several problems Ghana is facing some of which are due to a perverse culture, but others are rooted in weak institutions. By perverse culture, we side with Karl Marx and Huntington and condemn a culture that does not promote "thrift, hard work, education and discipline." I disagree with scholars who claim that solutions to Ghana's problems must accommodate Ghana's culture.

I asked why must we tolerate a culture of tardiness, indiscipline, filth and carelessness. Why should we say "enye hwee" translated to mean "it does not matter" to every situation that is wrong in Ghana? Why so much apathy? Surely, we can do better. The effective solution here to me seems to be education and credible leadership with integrity that can transform these cultural traits however long it takes. This will enable the culture to promote strong institution which will then result in a progressive culture that is supportive of a virtuous cycle of prosperity.

The problems of weak institutions have to do with arrogating too much power in the hands of the executive and weak property rights. These problems are consistent with the influential literature on institutions which claim such weak institutions have a historical basis. These are linked with a historical rule of despotic regimes and they stimulate a perverse and unhelpful culture of sycophancy. This is true of Ghana and necessitates an over-haul of the constitutions as Armah (2016) has so carefully argued.

Chapter 3 addressed the culture and institution nexus and evaluated the inter-relationships between culture and institutions. These two concepts overlap and to combat corruption one must address both in a reinforcing way. It makes little sense to focus on formal institutions and ignore informal institutions or culture in an African country.

Weak institutions and a perverse culture are big problems, but they are only part of Africa's Challenge of Development. Africa, and Ghana, also suffers from weak leadership and an inability to replicate and develop new technology. Solving the cultural and institutional-related problems is a necessary first step, and the work should begin now.

Chapter 4 focused on the inter-relationships between culture and corruption as it applies to Ghana. It used short stories to describe how a culture of apathy that has seeped into Ghanaian economic realities is creating opportunities for corruption and making the development challenge harder to confront. It discussed the literature suggestions about how to handle perverse culture that seems to nurture corruption and hamper growth. The chapter then identified the limitations of the literature suggestions and identified plausible alternatives that offer more pragmatic avenues for limiting corruption by directly trying to undermine or change perverse cultural practices through changing mindsets via education, leadership with integrity and the smart use of technology.

BIBLIOGRAPHY

Armah, S. E. (2016). Strategies to Stimulate Ghana's Economic Transformation and Diversification. *Ashesi Economics Lecture Series Journal, 2*(1), 9–16.

Huntington, S. (2000). *Political Order in Changing Societies.* New Haven: Yale University Press.

Landes, D. (2000). Culture Makes Almost All the Difference. In *Culture Matters: How Values Shape Human Progress* (pp. 2–13). New York: Basic Books.

Bibliography

Acemoglu, D., Johnson, S., & Robinson, J. A. (2001). The Colonial Origins of Comparative Development: An Empirical Investigation. *American Economic Review, 91*(5), 1369–1401.

Acemoglu, D., Johnson, S., & Robinson, J. A. (2006, December). The Colonial Origins of Comparative Development: An Empirical Investigation. *American Economic Review, 91*, 1369–1401.

Achim, M. V. (2016). Cultural Dimension of Corruption: A Cross-Country Survey. *International Advances in Economic Research, 22*, 333–345.

Adei, S., & Armah, S. E. A. (2018). *"Ghana Beyond Aid" and What It Will Take to Achieve It.* Paper Presented at Ashesi Econ Lecture Series, Norton-Motulsky Hall, King Engineering Building, Ashesi University, Berekuso, E/R, Ghana.

Ades, A., & Di Tella, R. (1999). Rents, Competition, and Corruption. *American Economic Review, 89*(4), 982–993.

Adjaye, J. K. (1987). Time, the Calendar, and History Among the Akan of Ghana. *The Journal of Ethnic Studies, 15*(3), 71.

Ahmed, A. (2018). Criminal Cases in Graft Scandal Stifled in Mexico – Mexico Could Press Bribery Charges. It Just Hasn't. *The New York Times*, p. A1. Available at https://www.nytimes.com/2018/06/11/world/americas/mexico-odebrecht-investigation.html

Akpomuvie, O. B. (2010). Culture and the Challenges of Development in Africa: Towards A Hybridization of Traditional and Modern Values. *African Research Review, 4*(1), 288–297.

Alam, M. S. (1995). A Theory of Limits on Corruption and Some Applications. *Kyklos, 48*, 419–435.

Alatas, et al. (2009, January). Gender, Culture, and Corruption: Insights from an Experimental Analysis. *Southern Economic Journal, 75*(3), 663–680.

Alesina, A., & Giuliano, P. (2015). Culture and Institutions. *Journal of Economic Literature, 53*(4), 898–944.

Alhassan-Alolo, N. (2007). Gender and Corruption: Testing the New Consensus. *Public Administration and Development, 27*, 227–237.

Algan, Y., & Cahuc, P. (2014). Trust, Growth, and Well-Being: New Evidence and Policy Implications. In P. Aghion & S. N. Durlauf (Eds.), *Handbook of Economic Growth* (Vol. 2A, pp. 49–120). Amsterdam/San Diego: Elsevier, North-Holland.

Ampratwum, E. F. (1987). The Fight Against Corruption and Its Implications for Development in Developing and Transition Economies. *Journal of Money Laundering Control, 11*(1), 76–87.

Andah, B. W., & Bolarinwa, K. (1994). *A Celebration of Africa's Roots and Legacy*. Ibadan: Fajee Publishers Ltd.

Andvig, J. C., & Moene, K. O. (1990). How Corruption May Corrupt. *Journal of Economic Behavior and Organization, 13*, 63–76.

Annan, K. (2004). *Statement by the Secretary General on the Adoption by the General Assembly of the United Nations (UN) Convention Against Corruption*. New York: The United Nations Office on Drugs and Crime (UNODOC).

Armah, S. E. (2016). Strategies to Stimulate Ghana's Economic Transformation and Diversification. *Ashesi Economics Lecture Series Journal, 2*(1), 9–16.

Arrow, K. J. (1972). Gifts and Exchanges. *Philosophy & Public Affairs, 1*, 343–362.

Aryeetey, E., & Kanbur, R. (2016). *The Economy of Ghana Sixty Years After Independence*. Oxford: Oxford University Press.

Ashraf, Q., & Galor, O. (2007). *Cultural Assimilation, Cultural Diffusion and the Origin of the Wealth of Nations* (Working paper). Providence: Brown University.

Banerjee, A. (1999). A Theory of Misgovernance. *Quarterly Journal of Economics, 112*(4), 1289–1332. 1997.

Banerjee, A. V., & Duflo, E. (2007). The Economic Lives of the Poor. *The Journal of Economic Perspectives, 21*(1), 141–167.

Banfield, E. (1958). *The Moral Basis of a Backward Society*. New York: Simon and Schuster.

Banfield, E. C. (1985). Corruption as a Feature of Governmental Organization. In *Here the People Rule* (pp. 147–170). Boston: Springer.

Bardhan, P. (1997). Corruption and Development: A Review of Issues. *Journal of Economic Literature, 35*, 1320–1346.

Barr, A., & Serra, D. (2010). Corruption and Culture: An Experimental Analysis. *Journal of Public Economics, 94*(2010), 862–869.

Barro, R. J. (1991, May). Economic Growth in a Cross Section of Countries. *Quarterly Journal of Economics, 106*(2), 407–443.

Barro, R., & Lee, J.-W. (2001). International Data on Educational Attainment: Updates and Implications. *Oxford Economic Papers, 3*, 541–563.

Barro, R. J., & McCleary, R. (2003). *Religion and Economic Growth* (No. w9682). National Bureau of Economic Research.
Bates, R. H. (2006). Institutions and Development. *Journal of African Economies, 15*(Suppl. 1), 10–61.
Bauer, P. T. (1972). *Dissent on Development: Studies and Debates in Development Economics*. Cambridge, MA: Harvard University Press.
Baumol, W. (1990). Entrepreneurship: Productive, Unproductive and Destructive. *The Journal of Political Economy, 98*(5), 893–921.
Beck, P. J., & Maher, M. W. (1986). A Comparison of Bribery and Bidding in Thin Markets. *Economics Letters, 20*(1), 1–5.
Becker, G. (1964). *Human Capital: A Theoretical and Empirical Analysis, with Special Reference to Education*. New York: National Bureau of Economic Research.
Becker, G. S., & Stigler, G. J. (1974). Law Enforcement, Malfeasance, and Compensation of Enforcers. *The Journal of Legal Studies, 3*(1), 1–18.
BeNer, A., & Putterman, L. (1998). Values, Institutions, and Economics. *The Good Society, 8*(2), 14–16.
Bisin, A., & Verdier, T. (2000). "Beyond the Melting Pot": Cultural Transmission, Marriage, and the Evolution of Ethnic and Religious Traits. *The Quarterly Journal of Economics, 115*(3), 955–988.
Bisin, A., & Verdier, T. (2001). The Economics of Cultural Transmission and the Dynamics of Preferences. *Journal of Economic Theory, 97*(2), 298–319.
Bontis, N., & Seleim, A. (2009). The Relationship between Culture and Corruption: A Cross-National Study. *Journal of Intellectual Capital, 10*(1), 165–184. https://doi.org/10.1108/14691930910922978.
Bowman, M. (1966). The Human Investment Revolution in Economic Thought. *Sociology of Education, 39*(2), 111. https://doi.org/10.2307/2111863.
Boyd, R., & Richerson, P. J. (1985). *Culture and the Evolutionary Process*. Chicago: University of Chicago Press.
Boyd, R., & Richerson, P. J. (2005). *The Origin and Evolution of Cultures*. Oxford: Oxford University Press.
Braun, M., & Di Tella, R. (2002). *Inflation and Corruption*. Harvard Business School, mimeo.
British Broadcasting Corporation (BBC). (2018). *The Yemen Crisis in 400 Words*. https://www.bbc.com/news/world-middle-east-44466574
Burbach, T. (2016, September 22). *The Coming Peace: Africa's Declining Conflicts, Oxford Research Group*. https://www.oxfordresearchgroup.org.uk/blog/the-coming-peace-africas-declining-conflicts
Cable News Network (CNN). (2019, April). Enron Fast Facts. *CNN Library*. https://edition.cnn.com/2013/07/02/us/enron-fast-facts/index.html
Cameron, L., Chaudhuri, A., Erkal, N., & Gangadharan, L. (2009). Propensities to Engage in and Punish Corrupt Behavior: Experimental Evidence from Australia, India, Indonesia and Singapore. *Journal of Public Economics, 93*(7–9), 843–851.

Cass, D. (1965). Optimum Growth in an Aggregative Model of Capital Accumulation. *Review of Economic Studies, 32*, 233–240.

Cerqueti, R., Coppier, R., & Piga, G. J. (2012). Corruption, Growth and Ethnic Fractionalization: A Theoretical Model. *Journal of Economics, 106*(2), 153–181.

Clague, C., Knack, S., & Gleason, S. (2001). Determinants of Lasting Democracy in Poor Countries: Culture, Development, and Institutions. *The Annals of the American Academy of Political and Social Science, 573*(1), 16–41.

Coleman, J. S. (1990). *Foundations of Social Theory*. Cambridge, MA: Harvard University Press.

Davis, J. H., & Ruhe, J. A. (2003). Perceptions of Country Corruption: Antecedents and Outcomes. *Journal of Business Ethics, 43*(4), 275–288.

De Soto, H. (2000). *The Mystery of Capital: Why Capitalism Triumphs in the West and Fails Everywhere Else*. New York: Basic Books.

Doepke, M., & Zilibotti, F. (2008). Occupational Choice and the Spirit of Capitalism. *The Quarterly Journal of Economics, 123*(2), 747–793.

Dollar, D., Fisman, R., & Gatti, R. (2001). Are Women Really the "Fairer" Sex? Corruption and Women in Government. *Journal of Economic Behavior and Organization, 46*(4), 423–429.

Domar, E. (1946). Capital Expansion, Rate of Growth and Employment. *Econometrica, 14*(2), 137–147. https://doi.org/10.2307/1905364. JSTOR1905364.

Dreher, A., Kotsogiannis, C., & McCorriston, S. (2007). Corruption Around the World: Evidence from a Structural Model. *Journal of Comparative Economics, 35*, 443–466.

Durlauf, S. (2018). *Institutions, Development and Growth: Where Does Evidence Stand*. Economic Development and Institutions Working Paper 18, 4.

Edward, B. (1958). The Moral Basis of a Backward Society. *Glencoe, 111*, 85.

Fang, T. (2003). A Critique of Hofstede's Fifth National Cultural Dimension. *International Journal of Cross Cultural Management, 3*(3), 347–368.

Fernández, R. (2013). Cultural Change as Learning: The Evolution of Female Labor Force Participation over a Century. *American Economic Review, 103*(1), 472–500.

Fernández, R., & Fogli, A. (2009). Culture: An Empirical Investigation of Beliefs, Work, and Fertility. *American Economic Journal: Macroeconomics, 1*(1), 146–177.

Fernández, R., Fogli, A., & Olivetti, C. (2004). Mothers and Sons: Preference Formation and Female Labor Force Dynamics. *The Quarterly Journal of Economics, 119*(4), 1249–1299.

Fisman, R., & Miguel, E. (2007). Corruption, Norms, and Legal Enforcement: Evidence from Diplomatic Parking Tickets. *Journal of Political Economy, 115*(6), 1020–1048.

Fukuyama, F. (1995). *Trust: The Social Virtues and the Creation of Prosperity* (Vol. 99). New York: Free Press.

Gambetta, D. (1988). Fragments of an Economic Theory of the Mafia. *European Journal of Sociology/Archives Européennes de Sociologie, 29*(1), 127–145.

Gardner, F. (2011). How the Arab Spring Begun. *The BBC.* https://www.bbc.com/news/av/world-middle-east-16212447/how-the-arab-spring-began

Gatti, R., Paternostro, S., & Rigolini, J. (2003, August). *Individual Attitudes Toward Corruption: Do Social Effects Matter?* World Bank Policy Research Working Paper 3122.

Getz, K. A., & Volkema, R. J. (2001). Culture, Perceived Corruption, and Economics. *Business and Society, 40*(1), 7–31.

Ghanaweb. (2018). *Woyome Settles ₵4.6m of ₵51m Debt.* https://www.ghanaweb.com/GhanaHomePage/NewsArchive/Woyome-settles-4-6m-of-51m-debt-676381

Ghanaweb. (2019, September 16). Apologize to Ghanaians for Dashing Bauxite to Your Brother – NPP Tells Mahama. *Ghanaweb.* https://www.ghanaweb.com/GhanaHomePage/NewsArchive/Apologize-to-Ghanaians-for-dashing-bauxite-to-your-brother-NPP-tells-Mahama-781362

Giuliano, P. (2007). Living Arrangements in Western Europe: Does Cultural Origin Matter? *Journal of the European Economic Association, 5*(5), 927–952.

Glynn, P., Kobrin, S. J., & Naim, M. (1997). The Globalization of Corruption. *Corruption and the Global Economy, 7*, 17.

Goodstein, L. D., Hunt, J. W., & Hofstede, G. (1981). Commentary: Do American Theories Apply Abroad? *Organizational Dynamics, 10*(1), 49–68.

Gorodnichenko, Y., & Roland, G. (2011). Which Dimensions of Culture Matter for Long-Run Growth? *American Economic Review, 101*(3), 492–498. https://doi.org/10.1257/aer.101.3.492.

Gorodnichenko, Y., & Roland, G. (2017). Culture, institutions, and the wealth of nations. *Review of Economics and Statistics, 99*(3), 402–416.

Gould, D. J. (1991). Administrative Corruption: Incidence, Causes and Remedial Strategies. In A. Farazmand (Ed.), *Handbook of Comparative and Development Public Administration.* New York: Marcel Dekker.

Granato, J., Inglehart, R., & Leblang, D. (1996). The Effect of Cultural Values on Economic Development: Theory, Hypotheses, and Some Empirical Tests. *American Journal of Political Science, 40*, 607–631.

Greif, A. (1994). Cultural Beliefs and the Organization of Society: A Historical and Theoretical Reflection on Collectivist and Individualist Societies. *Journal of Political Economy, 102*(5), 912–950.

Greif, A. (2006a). Family Structure, Institutions, and Growth: The Origins and Implications of Western Corporations. *American Economic Review, 96*(2), 308–312.

Greif, A. (2006b). *Institutions and the Path to the Modern Economy: Lessons from Medieval Trade*. Cambridge: Cambridge University Press.

Greif, A., & Tabellini, G. (2010). Cultural and Institutional Bifurcation: China and Europe Compared. *American Economic Review, 100*(2), 135–140.

Guiso, L., Sapienza, P., & Zingales, L. (2006). Does Culture Affect Economic Outcomes? *Journal of Economic Perspectives, 20*(2), 23–48.

Guiso, L., Sapienza, P., & Zingales, L. (2008). Social Capital as Good Culture. *Journal of the European Economic Association, 6*(2–3), 295–320.

Guiso, L., Sapienza, P., & Zingales, L. (2015). Corporate Culture, Societal Culture, and Institutions. *American Economic Review, 105*(5), 336–339.

Halkos, G. E., & Tzeremes N. G. (2011). *Investigating the Cultural Patterns of Corruption: A Nonparametric Analysis*. MPRA Munich Personal RePEc Archive.

Hall, R. E., & Jones, C. I. (1999). Why Do Some Countries Produce So Much More Output Per Worker Than Others? *The Quarterly Journal of Economics, 114*(1), 83–116.

Harrison, L. E., & Huntington, S. P. (Eds.). (2000). *Culture Matters: How Values Shape Human Progress*. New York: Basic Books.

Harrod, R. F. (1939). An Essay in Dynamic Theory. *The Economic Journal, 49*(193), 14–33. https://doi.org/10.2307/2225181.JSTOR2225181.

Hasty, J. (2005). The Pleasures of Corruption: Desire and Discipline in Ghanaian Political Culture. *Cultural Anthropology, 20*(2), 271–301.

Hauk, E., & Saez-Marti, M. (2002). On the Cultural Transmission of Corruption. *Journal of Economic Theory, 107*(2), 311–335.

Heffner, F. (2002). The Role of Beliefs and Cultural Attitudes in Economic Development. *The Review of Regional Studies, 32*(1), 1–8.

Herald. (2018, November 1). *Maritime Boss Fixes 11 Air-Conditioners in Gov't Bungalow*. http://theheraldghana.com/maritime-boss-fixes-11-air-conditioners-in-govt-bungalow/

Hofstede, G. (1980). *Culture's Consequences: International Differences in Work-Related Values*. Beverly Hills: Sage Publishers.

Hofstede, G. (1986). Cultural Differences in Teaching and Learning. *International Journal of Intercultural Relations, 10*(3), 301–320.

Hofstede, G. (1990). *Cultures and Organizations: Software of the Mind*. London: McGraw-Hill.

Hofstede, G. (1994). Cultural and Other Difference in Teaching and Learning. In A. van der Walt (Ed.), *The Principles of Multicultural Tertiary Education* (pp. 71–79).

Hofstede, G. (2001). *Culture's Consequences: Comparing Values, Behaviours, Institutions, and Organizations Across Nations* (2nd ed.). Thousand Oaks: Sage.

Hofstede, G. (2006). What Did GLOBE Really Measure? Researchers' Minds Versus Respondents' Minds. *Journal of International Business Studies, 37*, 882–896.

Hofstede, G. (2010). The GLOBE Debate: Back to Relevance. *Journal of International Business Studies, 41*, 1339–1346.

Hofstede, G., & Bond, M. H. (1988). The Confucius Connection: From Cultural Roots to Economic Growth. *Organizational Dynamics, 16*, 4–21.

Hofstede, G., & Hofstede, G. J. (2005). *Cultures and Organizations: Software of the Mind* (Rev. 2nd ed.). New York: McGraw-Hill. For Translations, See https://www.geerthofstede.nl and "Our Books".

Hofstede, G., & McCrae, R. R. (2004). Culture and Personality Revisited: Linking Traits and Dimensions of Culture. *Cross-Cultural Research, 38*, 52–88.

Hofstede, G., & Minkov, M. (2011). The Evolution of Hofstede's Doctrine. *Cross Cultural Management: An International Journal, 18*(1), 10–20.

Hofstede, G., Neuijen, B., Ohayv, D. D., & Sanders, G. (1990). Measuring Organizational Cultures: A Qualitative and Quantitative Study Across Twenty Cases. *Administrative Science Quarterly, 35*, 286–316.

Hofstede, G., Hofstede, G. H., & Arrindell, W. A. (1998a). *Masculinity and Femininity: The Taboo Dimension of National Cultures* (Vol. 3). Thousand Oaks: Sage.

Hofstede, G., Arrindell, W. A., Best, D. L., de Mooij, M., Hoppe, M. H., van de Vliert, E., van Rossum, J. H. A., Verweij, J., Vunderink, M., & Williams, J. E. (1998b). *Masculinity and Femininity: The Taboo Dimension of National Cultures*. Thousand Oaks: Sage.

Hofstede, G., Hofstede, G. J., & Minkov, M. (2005). *Cultures and Organizations: Software of the Mind* (Vol. 2). New York: McGraw-Hill.

Hofstede, G., Hofstede, G. J., & Minkov, M. (2010). *Cultures and Organizations: Software of the Mind*. New York: McGraw.

Hofstede, G., Hofstede, G. J., & Minkov, M. (2010). *Cultures and Organizations: Software of the Mind* (Rev. 3rd ed.). New York: McGraw-Hill. For Translations, See https://www.geerthofstede.nl and "Our Books".

Huntington, S. (2000). *Political Order in Changing Societies*. New Haven: Yale University Press.

Huntington, S. P., & Harrison, L. E. (2000). *Culture matters: How values shape human progress*. New York: Basic Books.

Husted, B. (1999). Corruption and Culture. *Journal of International Business Studies, 30*(2), 339. 2nd Qtr.

Inglehart, R., & Baker, W. E. (2000). Modernization, Cultural Change, and the Persistence of Traditional Values. *American Sociological Review, 65*(1), 19–51.

Islam, N. (1995). Growth Empirics: A Panel Data Approach. *Quarterly Journal of Economics, 110*, 1127–1170.

Jarrett, A. (1996). *The Under-Development of Africa: Colonialism, Neo-Colonialism and Socialism*. Lanham/New York/London: University Press of America.

Jiang, T., & Nie, H. (2014). The Stained China Miracle: Corruption, Regulation, and Firm Performance. *Economics Letters, 123*, 366–369.

Kaufmann, D. (1997). *Corruption: The Facts* (pp. 114–131). Available at www.Jstor.org/. Accessed 13 Nov 2006.

Kaufmann, D., & Wei, S. J. (1999). *Does "Grease Money" Speed Up the Wheels of Commerce?* (No. w7093). National Bureau of Economic Research.

Kirkman, B. L., Lowe, K. B., & Gibson, C. B. (2006). A Quarter Century of Culture's Consequences: A Review of Empirical Research Incorporating Hofstede's Cultural Values Framework. *Journal of International Business Studies, 37*(3), 285.

Klitgaard, R. (1988). *Controlling Corruption.* Berkeley/Los Angeles: University of California Press.

Klitgaard, R. (1991). *Controlling Corruption.* Berkeley/Los Angeles: University of California Press.

Klitgaard, R. (2017, June 13). *On Corruption and Culture.* Paper Presented at the Public Integrity and Anti-Corruption Workshop at Nuffield College, Oxford.

Knack, S., & Keefer, P. (1997). Does Social Capital Have an Economic Payoff? A Cross-Country Investigation. *The Quarterly Journal of Economics, 112*(4), 1251–1288.

Koopmans, T. C. (1965). On the Concept of Optimal Economic Growth. In *(Study Week on the) Econometric Approach to Development Planning, Chapter 4* (pp. 225–287). Amsterdam: North-Holland Publishing.

Krueger, A. O. (1974). The Political Economy of the Rent-Seeking Society. *The American Economic Review, 64*(3), 291–303.

La Porta, R., Lopez-de-Silanes, F., Shleifer, A., & Vishny, R. W. (1997). Trust in Large Organizations. *American Economic Review Papers and Proceedings, 87*, 333–338.

Landes, D. (1998). *Culture Matters: How Values Shape Human Progress*, L. E. Harrison & Samuel P. Huntington (Eds.), 2000. New York: Basic Books.

Landes, D. (2000). Culture Makes Almost All the Difference. In *Culture Matters: How Values Shape Human Progress* (pp. 2–13). New York: Basic Books.

Lanier, C., & Kirshner, M. (2018). Corruption and Culture: Empirical Analysis of Long-Term Indulgence and Corrupt Systems. *The Review of Business, and Interdisciplinary Journal on Risk and Society, 38*(2), 30–43.

Leff, N. H. (1964). Economic Development Through Bureaucratic Corruption. *American Behavioral Scientist, 8*(3), 8–14.

Lewis, W. A. (1954). Econ Development with Unlimited Supplies of Labor. *The Manchester School of Economic and Social Studies, 22*, 139–192.

Lien, D. H. D. (1986). A Note on Competitive Bribery Games. *Economics Letters, 22*(4), 337–341.

Lipset, S. M., & Lenz, G. S. (2000). Corruption, Culture, and Markets. In L. E. Harrison & S. P. Huntington (Eds.), *Culture Matters: How Values Shape Human Progress* (pp. 112–125). New York: Basic Books.

Lopez-Claros, A., & Perotti, V. (2014). *Does Culture Matter for Development?* Policy Research Working Paper No. WPS 7092. Washington, DC: World Bank Group.

Lucas, R. (1988). On the Mechanics of Economic Development. *Journal of Monetary Economics, 22,* 3–42.

Lucas, Robert E., Jr. (1990). Why Doesn't Capital Flow from Rich to Poor Countries? *The American Economic Review, 80*(2), Papers and Proceedings of the Hundred and Second Annual Meeting of the American Economic Association, pp. 92–96.

Manasseh, A. (2016, June). *Full Story: President Mahama's 'Gift' from Burkinabe Contractor.* http://www.manassehazure.com/2016/06/full-story-president-mahamas-gift-burkinabe-contractor/

Mankiw, N. G., Romer, D., & Weil, D. N. (1992, May). Contribution to the Empirics of Economic Growth. *The Quarterly Journal of Economics, 107*(2), 407–437.

Mauro, P. (1995). Corruption and Growth. *The Quarterly Journal of Economics, 110*(3), 681–712.

Mbaku, J. M. (2019). Corruption and Economic Development. In E. Nnadozie & A. Jerome (Eds.), *African Economic Development* (2nd ed., pp. 331–345). Bingley, England: Emerald Publishers.

McLaughlin, E. (2013). Culture and Corruption: An Explanation of the Differences Between Scandinavia and Africa, American International Journal of Research in Humanities. *Arts and Social Sciences, 2*(2), 85–91.

Minkov, M. (2007). *What Makes Us Different and Similar: A New Interpretation of the World Values and Other Cross-Cultural Data.* Sofia: Klasika i Stil Publishing House.

Minkov, M. (2011). *Cultural Differences in a Globalizing World.* London: Emerald Group Publishing.

Minkov, M., & Blagoev, V. (2009). Cultural Values Predict Subsequent Economic Growth. *International Journal of Cross-Cultural Management, 9*(1), 5–24.

Mohammad, S., & Husted, B. W. (2019). Law Abiding Organizational Climates in Developing Countries: The Role of Institutional Factors and Socially Responsible Organizational Practices. *Business Ethics: A European Review, 2019,* 118. https://doi.org/10.1111/beer.12228.

Murdoch, A. (2009). How Much Culture Is There in Corruption? Some Thoughts on Transformation-Cum-Collective Culture Shock in Post-Communist Poland. *Journal of Intercultural Management, 1*(1), 42–63.

Murdock, G. P. (1965). *Culture and Society: Twenty-Four Essays.* Pittsburgh: University of Pittsburgh Press.

Murphy, K. M., Shleifer, A., & Vishny, R. W. (1991). The Allocation of Talent: Implications for Growth. *The Quarterly Journal of Economics, 106*(2), 503–530.

Myjoyonline. (2018, June 28). *The 1979 Killing of Army Generals Unjustifiable; Activist 'Confesses' After 39 yrs*. https://www.myjoyonline.com/politics/2018/June-28th/1979-killing-of-army-generals-unjustifiable-activist-confesses-after-39yrs.php

Ndulu, B. J., & O'Connell, S. A. (2000). Correction: Governance and Growth in Sub-Saharan Africa. *Journal of Economic Perspectives, 14*(3), 241–242.

Ndulu, B. J., & O'Connell, S. A. (2007). Policy Plus: African Economic Growth, 1960–2000 (Chapter 1). In B. J. Ndulu & S. A. O'Connell (Eds.), *The Political Economy of Economic Growth in Africa, 1960–2000*. Cambridge: Cambridge University Press.

Njoh, A. (2006). *Tradition, Culture and Development in Africa Historical Lessons for Modern Development Planning*. London: Routledge.

Nkrumah, K. (1961). *I Speak of Freedom: A Statement of African Ideology*. New York: Praeger.

Nnadozie, E., & Afeikhena, J. (Eds.). (2019). *African Economic Development*. New York: Emerald Publishers.

North, D. (1990). *Institutions, Institutional Change, and Economic Performance*. New York: Cambridge University Press.

North, D. (1991). Institutions. *Journal of Economic Perspective, 5*(1), 97–112.

North, D. (2005). *Understanding the Process of Economic Change*. Princeton: Princeton University Press.

North, D., & Thomas, R. P. (1973). *The Rise of the Western World: A New Economic History*. New York: Cambridge University Press.

North, D., Wallis, J. J., & Weingast, B. R. (2009). *Violence and Social Orders: A Conceptual Framework for Interpreting Recorded Human History*. Cambridge: Cambridge University Press.

Nye, J. S. (1967). Corruption and Political Development: A cost-benefit analysis. *American political science review, 61*(2), 417–427.

Odhiambo, E. S. (2002). The Cultural Dimensions of Development in Africa. *African Studies Review, 45*(3), 1–16.

Olivier de Sardan, Jean-Pierre. (1999). A Moral Economy of Corruption? *Journal of Modern African Studies, 37*(1), 25–52.

Olken, B. A. (2007). Monitoring Corruption: Evidence from a Field Experiment in Indonesia. *Journal of Political Economy, 115*(2), 200–249.

Platteau, J. P. (2000). Does Africa Need Land Reform? In *Evolving Land Rights, Policy and Tenure in Africa* (pp. 51–74). London: IIED.

Putnam, R. (1993). Explaining Institutional Performance. In *Making Democracy Work* (pp. 83–120). Princeton: Princeton University Press.

Rodney, W. (1981). *How Europe Underdeveloped Africa*. Washington, DC: Howard University Press.

Rodrik, D. (2005). Growth Strategies. *Handbook of Economic Growth, 1*, 967–1014.

Roland, G. (2016, January). *Culture, Institutions and Development*. Namur January 2016 Conference.

Roland, Y. G. G., & Gorodnichenko, Y. Y. (2013). *Culture, Institutions and Democratization*. Berkeley: University of California Berkeley.

Romer, P. (1990). Human Capital and Growth: Theory and Evidence. *Carnegie Rochester Con Series on Public Policy, 32*, 251–286.

Rose-Ackerman, S. (1975). The Economics of Corruption. *Journal of Public Economics, 4*(2), 187–203.

Rose-Ackerman, S. (1978). *Corruption: A Study of Political Economy*. New York: Academic Press.

Rose-Ackerman, S. (1999). *Corruption and Government*. Cambridge: Cambridge University Press.

Rose-Ackerman, S. (2004). *The Challenge of Poor Governance and Corruption*. Especial 1 DIREITO GV L. Rev., p. 207.

Rostow, W. W. (1960). *The Stages of Growth: A Non-Communist Manifesto* (pp. 4–16). Cambridge: Cambridge University Press.

Sachs, J. D., & Warner, A. M. (2001). The Curse of Natural Resources. *European Economic Review, 45*(4–6), 827–838.

Sandholtz, W., & Gray, M. M. (2003). International Integration and National Corruption. *International Organization, 57*(4), 761–800.

Sandholtz, W., & Koetzle, W. (2000). Accounting for Corruption: Economic Structure, Democracy, and Trade. *International Studies Quarterly, 44*(1), 31–50.

Sandholtz, W., & Taagepera, R. (2005). Corruption, Culture, and Communism. *International Review of Sociology, 15*(1), 109–131.

Schleifer, A., & Vishny, R. W. (1993). Corruption. *Quarterly Journal of Economics, 108*(3), 599–617.

Schultz, T. W. (1960, December). Capital Formation by Education. *Journal of Political Economy, 68*, 571–583.

Schwartz, S. H. (1999). A Theory of Cultural Values and Some Implications for Work. *Applied Psychology, 48*(1), 23–47.

Scott, J. (1972). *Comparative Political Corruption*. Englewood Cliffs: Prentice-Hall.

Segal, T. (2019, May). *The Enron Scandal. The Fall of a Wallstreet Darling*. Laws and Regulation; Crime and Fraud. https://www.investopedia.com/updates/enron-scandal-summary/

Sen, A. (1999). *Development as Freedom*. Oxford. Oxford: Oxford University Press.

Serageldin, I., & Tabaroff, J. (1992). *Culture and Development in Africa*. Proceedings of the World Bank Conference on Africa NY, The World Bank.

Shadabi, L. (2013). The Impact of Religion on Corruption. *The Journal of Business Inquiry, 12*, 102–117.

Smith, D. J. (2007). *A Culture of Corruption: Everyday Deception and Popular Discontent in Nigeria*. Princeton: Princeton University Press.

Solow (1956). A Contribution to the Theory of Economic Growth. *Quarterly Journal of Economics, 70*(1), 65–94.

Sondergaard, M. (1994). Hofstede's Consequences: A Study of Reviews, Citations, and Replications. *Organization Studies, 15*(3), 447–456.

Straus, S. (2012). Wars Do End! Changing Patterns of Political Violence in Sub-Saharan Africa. *African Affairs, 111*(443), 179–201.

Strykker, R. (2019, September 9). Why 'Not Ghana Beyond Corruption' – Dutch Ambassador Asks. *Myjoyonline News.* https://www.myjoyonline.com/politics/2019/September-6th/why-not-ghana-beyond-corruption-dutch-ambassador-asks.php

Swamy, A., Knack, S., Lee, Y., & Azfar, O. (2001). Gender and Corruption. *Journal of Development Economics, 64,* 25–55.

Swan, T. (1956). Economic Growth and Capital Accumulation. *Economic Record, 32*(63), 334–361.

Tabellini, G. (2007). Institutions and Culture IGIR Working Paper 330, University of Bocconi, Italy.

Tabellini, G. (2008). Institutions and Culture. *Journal of the European Economic Association, 6*(2–3), 255–294.

Tabellini, G. (2010). Culture and Institutions: Economic Development in the Regions of Europe. *Journal of the European Economic Association, 8*(4), 677–716.

Tanzi, V. (1998). Corruption Around the World: Causes, Consequences, Scope, and Cures. *Staff Papers, 45*(4), 559–594.

Taras, V., Kirkman, B. L., & Steel, P. (2010). Examining the Impact of Culture's Consequences: A Three-Decade, Multilevel, Meta-Analytic Review of Hofstede's Cultural Value Dimensions. *Journal of Applied Psychology, 95*(3), 405–439.

Tay, L., Herian, M. N., & Diener, E. (2014). Detrimental Effects of Corruption and Subjective Well-Being: Whether, How and When. *Social Psychological and Personality Science, 5*(7), 751–759.

Teixeira, A. A. C., Pimenta, C., Maia, A., & Moreira, J. A. (2016). *Corruption, Economic Growth and Globalization.* New York: Routledge.

Todaro, M. P., & Smith, S. C. (2006). *Economic Development* (8th ed.). Manila: Pearson South Asia Pte. Ltd..

Tong, W. (2014). Analysis of Corruption from Sociocultural Perspectives. *International Journal of Business and Social Science, 5*(11), 1–19.

Treisman, D. (2000). The Causes of Corruption: A Cross-National Study. *Journal of Public Economics, 76*(3), 399–457.

Waterbury, J. (1973). Endemic and Planned Corruption in a Monarchical Regime. *World Politics, 25*(4), 533–555.

Webber, R. A. (Ed.). (1969). *Culture and Management.* Homewood: Irwin.

Weber, M. (1930). *The Protestant Ethic and the Spirit of Capitalism.* NY Scribner.

Weber, M. (1970). *Essays in Sociology,* H. H. Gerth, & C. W. Mills (Eds.). London: Routledge & Kegan Paul. [Original Work Published 1948].

Weber, M. (1976). *The Protestant Ethic and the Spirit of Capitalism*. London: George Allen & Unwin. [Original Work Published 1930].

Wiki. (2019). Death of Brigadier Emmauel Kwasi Kotoka. In Wikipedia. Assessed 5 Jan 2020.

Wines, W. A., & Napier, N. K. (1992). Toward an Understanding of Cross-Cultural Ethics: A Tentative Model. *Journal of Business Ethics, 11*, 831–841.

World Bank. (1993). *The East Asian Miracle: Economic Growth and Public Policy* (pp. 611–638). Washington, DC/Dordrecht: World Bank Economics/Springer.

Yeganeh, H. (2013). *The Cultural Antecedents of Corruption: A Cross-national Study*. International Conference of HEI: State Capitalism in the New Global Political Economy. Quebec, Canada

Yew, L. K. (2000). *From Third World to First: The Singapore Story, 1965–2000: Singapore and the Asian Economic Boom*. New York: HarperCollins Publishers.

Index

A
Acemoglu, D., 5, 18, 47, 65, 70–72
Acheampong, Ignatius Kutu (Colonel), 38
Achim, M. V., 63
Addo, Nana (President), 35
Adei, S., 2
African Cup of Nations, 43
African development, 21, 23
Afrifa, Akwasi (Brigadier), 38
Afrifa, Akwasi (General), 40
Afro-barometer survey, 13
Agbesi Woyome, 41
Ahmed, A., 63
Air Vice Marshal George Yaw Boakye, 39
Akans, 44
Akpomuvie, 24
Akuffo, Fred (General), 38, 39
Alesina, A., 23–25, 28, 44, 45, 47, 64
Andah, B. W., 27
Ankrah, Joseph Arthur (Major General), 39
Annan, Kofi, 45
Antimarket, 3

Apathy, 14, 51, 52, 56, 61, 84
Arab Spring, 36
Armah, S. E. A., 2, 51
Armed Forces Revolutionary Council (AFRC), 39, 40
Arrow, K. J., 30
Arthathastra, 45
Aryeetey, E., 36
Assets, 16
Australia, 43
Autocratic demands, 51
Autocratic regime, 51

B
Baland, 29
Banerjee, A., 45
Banerjee, A. V., 15
Banfield, E., 24, 30, 65, 66
Banfield, E. C., 44
Bardhan, P., 45, 66
Barro, R. J., 25, 65
Bashir, Omar, 63
Bates, R. H., 36, 72
Battle of ideologies, 48

Bauer, Peter T., 22, 24
Becker, G. S., 44
Ben Ali, Zine al-Abidine, 63
Bener, A., 30
Benign dictator, 52
Bible, 49
Bisin, A., 25
The Black Stars, 43
Boahen, Adu (Professor), 40
Bolarinwa, K., 27
Bontis, N., 31
Botswana, 37, 38
Bouazizi, Mohamed, 63
Bouteflika, Abdelaziz, 63
Boyd, R., 27
Bribes, 12, 41, 52, 57, 63
Broadcasting Corporation (BBC), 1
Burbach, T., 36
Burkina Faso, 42
Busia, Kofi Abrefa (President), 38, 39

C

Captain Boakye-Gyan, 39
Chiefs, 10
China, 30, 31
Chinese Galamsey, 42
Church, 14, 15, 57, 60
Civilian democratic rule, 47
Civilian rule, 50, 51
CNN, 36
Col. Roger J. Felli, 39
Cold War, 48, 50
Cold War dynamics, 48
Coleman, J. S., 30
Collateral, 16
Colonel Emmanuel Kotoka, 39
Colonization, 16, 17, 22, 72
Commercial peddler, 52
Commonwealth Games, 43
Congo, 36, 38, 70
Constitution, 16, 50
Convention People's Party (CPP), 38

Corruption and culture in Ghana, 35–73
Counterproductive, 3, 72
Coup d' etats, 36
Credit card, 16
Cultural
 basis, 4
 beliefs, 27
 determinant, 5
 difference, 2, 11, 12, 15–18, 23, 25–27, 29, 30, 43, 44, 46, 47, 49, 50, 59, 61, 64–70
 disposition, 5
 and self-inflicted problem, 1
Cultural divergence, 30
Culture, 2–6, 8, 14, 18, 19, 21–31, 35–73, 83, 84
Culture and development, 26
The curse of natural resources, 36

D

Daily Guide, 42
De Soto, Hernando, 16
Dead Capital, 16
Democracy, 14, 16, 38, 45, 47, 50, 52, 54
Democratization, 44
Desk-sitting service jobs, 48
Developmental
 challenges, efforts, objectives, outcomes, progress, struggle, 2, 3, 5, 6, 18, 19, 23, 44–46, 48, 49, 65
Developmental outcomes, 48
Discipline, 2, 8, 13, 14, 17, 46, 50, 54, 69, 73
Disorganized, 3, 47, 53
Doepke, M., 25
Domar, E., 64, 65
Driver and Licensing Authority (DVLA), 57
Dufflo, E., 15

Dum Sor, 42
Dumping of cheaper goods, 17
Durlauf, S., 24, 29

E
Eastern Europe, 49
Economic literature, 46
Economics of culture, 45
Economy, 2–4, 13, 22, 26, 73
Education, 2–4, 10, 15, 16, 25, 38, 47, 48, 50, 51, 60–62, 69, 73, 84
Effective leadership, 3, 15, 50, 51
Emmanuel Kotoka (Colonel), 39
Empathy, 51
Enron, 63
Entrepreneurial spirit, 4
Enye hwee, 14, 17, 18, 51–55
Ethnicities, 38
Europe, 30, 31

F
Family heads, 10, 13
Fantes, 14
Fernández, R., 26
First world facilities, 4
Fisman, R., 25, 45, 63, 64, 67, 68
Fogli, A., 26
Foreign aid, 2, 44, 46, 66
Fukuyama, F., 30, 68
Functioning democracy, 12, 47, 52
Funerals, 15, 16

G
Gambetta, D., 30
Gambia, 37
Gas, 44
GDP, 44
Ghana, 52, 53
Ghana beyond Aid agenda, 35
Ghana beyond Corruption, 36
Ghanaian Behavior, 7–19
Ghana Revenue Authority (GRA), 58
Ghana Revenue Service (GRA), 42
Ghanaweb, 41, 42
Gift giving to leaders and royalty, 43
Giuliano, P., 23–25, 28, 44, 45, 47, 64
Gleason, S., 23
Glynn, P., 36
Gorodnichenko, Y, 25, 30
Gould, 45
Gray, 36
Greif, A., 27, 30
Grief, A., 23
Guaido, Juan, 63
Guinea fowls, 42
Guiso, L., 44

H
Hall, R. E., 24, 25
Hands off attitude of economic theory, 45
Hard work, 2, 4, 17, 47, 50, 69, 73
Heffner, F., 23, 46, 69
Hein, 30
The Herald, 42
Hofstede, G., 22, 27, 30, 31, 45, 50
Holy water, 54
Human capital, 22, 65
Huntington, S., 2–4, 17, 22–24, 30, 46–51, 62, 64, 68, 69, 73
Husted, B. W., 31

I
Ibrahim Mahama, 42
Illegal gold mining, 42
Importer oligopsony power, 22
Incentives for corruption, 47
Income per capita, 2, 30
Individualism *vs* collectivism, 30

Indolent, 47
Inequality and poverty, 25
Inflation, 2
Informal sector, 13, 52, 53, 56, 58
Institutional economics, 18
Institutions and culture, 21–31
Integrity, 51
Investment, 2, 4, 15, 16, 47, 69, 73

J
Jarrett, A., 22, 24
Johnson, S., 5, 18, 47, 65, 70–72
Jones, C. I., 24, 25

K
Kagame, Paul, 26
Kanbur, R., 36
Kaufmann, D., 45
Kautiliya, 45
Keefer, P., 25, 30
Kenya, 17, 37
Kirkman, B. L., 31
Klitgaard, Robert, 23, 44
Knack, S., 23, 25, 30
Koetzle, 36
Kosovo, 49
Kotei, Robert (Major General), 39
Krobo Edusei, 38
Krueger, A. O., 44
Kufuor, John Agyekum, 1, 2
Kusuum gboo, 44

L
La Porta, R., 30
Laissez faire, 14, 17
Landes, D., 23
Lands commission, 13
Land tenure, 13, 17
Lanier, C., 31

Leadership, 50
Leff, N. H., 45, 65
Liberia, 36, 37
Liman, Hilla (President), 40
Literature on corruption, 62–69
Lopez-Claros, A., 3, 18, 27
Lucas, Robert, 35, 64

M
Maduro, Nicholas (President), 63
Mahama, John, 42, 43
Malawi, 37
Manasseh, 43
Math education, 48
Mauritius, 37, 38
Mauro, P., 45
McCleary, R., 25
Media freedom, 38
Miguel, E., 25, 45, 63, 64, 67, 68
Military coup d'états, 47
Military dictatorship, 13, 19, 50
Military rule, 16, 17, 19, 47, 50, 51, 57, 60
Mills, John (President), 41
Mindsets, 16, 71, 73, 84
Mineral resources, 36
Modernization theory, 25
Murdoch, A., 50
Murdock, G. P., 27
Myanmar, 49
Myjoyonline, 39

N
Naming ceremonies, 15
National Democratic Congress (NDC), 16, 40
Nationalism, 51
Ndulu, B. J., 36
Neocolonialism, 23
New Patriotic Party (NPP), 40

Nigeria, 17
Njoh, Abe, 24
Nkrumah, Kwame, 22, 38, 40, 48, 50
North Korea, 48
North, D., 18, 28
Norway, 36
Nwachukwu, 67
Nye, J. S., 36

O
Obroni, 8
O'Connell, S. A., 36
Odebrecht, 63
Odhiambo, E. S., 23
Olivetti, C., 26
Olken, B., 45
Operation Guitar Boy, 39
Organized crime, 45

P
Pan-Africanism, 38
Pandora's box, 14
Perotti, V., 3, 18
Perverse culture, 47
Platteau, J. P., 30
Police, 10, 12–14, 16, 37, 56–59
Policy advice, 46
Poor institutions, 17
Poverty, 3, 5, 25, 64
Power crisis, 42
Price control laws, 40
Principal agent theory of corruption, 44
Productivity-enhancing technology, 48
Productivity sapping traits, 2
Pro-market wealth creation, 2
Property rights, 17
Protestant cultural trait, 65
Provincial National Defense Council (PNDC), 16
Public monopoly, 57

Public sector, 2
Public trust, 51
Putnam, R., 25, 30, 65
Putterman, L., 30

Q
Quality education, 48

R
Rawlings, Jerry John, 13, 52
Real GDP per capita, 2, 3, 38, 46
Real GDP per capita income, 38
Real per capita income, 41
Rear Admiral Joy K. Amedume, 39
Richerson, P. J., 27
Robinson, J. A., 5, 18, 65
Rodney, W., 22, 24
Rodrik, D., 29
Roland, G., 5, 25, 27, 29, 30
Rose-Ackerman, S., 36, 44, 45
Rostow, W. W., 22, 24
Ruhe, 67
Rule of law, 11, 13, 17, 45
Rural-urban migration, 14
Rwanda, 17, 18, 26, 38

S
Sachs, J. D., 21, 36, 65
Sandholtz, W., 36
Sanitation problems, 12
Sapienza, P., 23
Saudi Arabia, 63
Schleifer, A., 44
Schwartz, Shalom, 30, 66
Scientific Socialism, 50
Seleim, A., 31
Serageldin, Ismael, 23
Short stories of Ghanaian traditon, 51–62

Sierra Leone, 36
Singapore, 26
Size of population, 2
Slavery, 16, 22
Slums, 11, 13, 17
Smith, Daniel Jordan, 37
Socialist country, 17
Solow, R. M., 24, 64
South Africa, 37
South Korea, 2–4, 46–49, 73
Steel, P., 31
STEM, 48
Stigler, G. J., 44
Straus, S., 36
Stryker, Ron, 35
Sub-Saharan Africa (SSA), 35, 37, 49
Sudan, 36

T
Tabaroff, 23
Tabellini, G., 18, 23, 24, 30, 62, 64, 66, 68
Tageepara, 36
Tanzi, 62
Taras, V., 31
Tardiness, 2, 4, 6
Technology, 26, 48, 51, 57, 73, 84
Terrorism, 45
The 31st December Revolution, 40
Thrift, 2, 17, 47, 50, 69, 73
Todaro, M. P., 25, 26
Traditional
  arrangement, 14
  ceremonies, 14
  cloth, 15
  culture, 14
  kente, 15
  leaders, 5
  practices, 14
  wedding, 14, 15
Transparency International's Corruption Perception Index (CPI), 38

Treisman, D., 36, 45
Tribal politics, 49
Tsalikis, 67
Tunisia, 36

U
Uganda, 37, 48
Undisciplined, 3, 47
Unemployment, 25
Union of Soviet Socialist Republic, 48
United Nations (UN), 45
USA, 48
Utuka, E. K. (Major General), 39

V
Verdier, T., 25
Viagra, 52
Vishny, R. W., 44
Voodoo, 53

W
Warner, A. M., 21, 36
Waterbury, J., 36
Weak institutions, 47
Wedding, 7, 8, 14–16
Winner takes all system, 17
World Bank, 36
Wulomo, 52

Y
Yao, 52
Yeganeh, H., 68
Yen sei amamere, 44
Yew, Lee Kwan, 26

Z
Zilibotti, F., 25
Zingales, L., 23

CPSIA information can be obtained
at www.ICGtesting.com
Printed in the USA
LVHW080208240220
647976LV00006B/104